CHOOSING LIFE

Dorothee Soelle

CHOOSING LIFE

FORTRESS PRESS   **PHILADELPHIA**

Translated by Margaret Kohl
from the German
Wählt das Leben
Kreuz Verlag, Stuttgart and Berlin 1980

Translation © SCM Press Ltd 1981

First American Edition by Fortress Press 1981

Library of Congress Cataloging in Publication Data

Soelle, Dorothee.
  Choosing life.

  Translation of: Wählt das Leben.
    1. Christianity and justice—Addresses, essays,
  lectures. 2. Christianity and politics—Addresses,
  essays, lectures. I. Title.
  BR115.J8S6413 1981   261.7   81-43082
  ISBN 0-8006-0667-1   AACR2

9017F81 Printed in the United States of America 1–667

CONTENTS

Author's Note   vi

Preface by Bishop Colin Winter   vii

1 Faith as a Struggle against Objective
  Cynicism   1

2 Sin and Estrangement   20

3 Cross and Liberation   47

4 Christ – the Dignity of Men and Women   61

5 Resurrection and Liberation   79

6 The Argentinian Context   98

  Notes   114

AUTHOR'S NOTE

The ideas in the first five chapters originated in a series of lectures which I gave in Buenos Aires in September 1979. In order to preserve the authenticity, I have avoided making any considerable alterations in the lecture style. Chapter 6 is a report on the political conditions I came to know in Argentina, and the content of this chapter is closely bound up with my theological ideas.

PREFACE

At the end of the 1939–45 war in Europe, a German pastor was travelling by train from London to Chichester to meet Bishop George Bell. He said in a BBC interview, after Bell's death, how he was seized with a sudden, overwhelming feeling of doubt as the train approached his destination. He found himself asking this frightening question, 'Is there such a person as George Bell? Does he really exist?' Recently released from a Nazi prison, he was travelling to thank the bishop who had stood by Dietrich Bonhoeffer, who had struggled valiantly to shorten the war, who had fearlessly declared that all Germans were not Nazis, who had dared condemn Churchill over the indiscriminate bombing of non-military German targets, who had been a forthright champion of justice at national and international level and was a committed ecumenist, able to rise above the pettiness and prejudices of denominationalism, but who was most manifestly a humble man of prayer and, therefore, a fighter for truth to the end. With all this concentrated in one person, was it any wonder that the pastor doubted Bell's very existence? In the period of total war, many Christians, both in Germany and England, had compromised so many imperatives of the gospel for varying reasons – some understandable, some pathetic, some plainly ignoble; Bonhoeffer and Bell were clearly not among their number. Compromise was not part of their Christian vocabulary – nor is it part of Dorothee Soelle's.

As I listened to Dorothee Soelle lecture at the Goethe

Institute in London I had pretty much the same reaction as the German pastor. How could such a person possibly exist in modern Germany? – the odds are so stacked against her. She gave a brilliant lecture and had an immediate impact on the audience. An academic among them asked a question almost ten minutes long, twisting and turning in tautology, and finally became ensnared in his own verbosity, playing intellectual badminton, with her as the shuttlecock. But soon violence erupted against her personally. She is a woman, a theologian and a Marxist – how more handicapped can one be addressing a middle-class German and English audience in London!

There is a cost to discipleship, as Bonhoeffer and Bell knew in their different ways: it is suffering. Dorothee Soelle has clearly experienced this because of what she is, what she says and where she is saying it. Yet in her whole being, and most markedly in her writing, she has clearly transcended the violence that surrounds her, and which seeks to destroy what she says and what she stands for. I learn from this and marvel at it. She never gives up: the propulsion here is that of the real Christian revolutionary; but the motivation is love.

> There are convincing reasons for despising people – there are excellent reasons for despising myself. He (Jesus) teaches me an infinite revolutionary YES which does not leave me anything or anybody at all.

Those who know her, or who have met her, as I have only briefly, will know and recognize in her the power of that love.

> I want to learn to be more loving; I want to be different from what I am; I want to diminish the distance between me and Christ; I want to live and realize righteousness, justice and love, the basic values of the Jewish and

viii

Christian tradition; I want to share in that tradition; I want to help to build the kingdom of God, in which righteousness, justice and love exist for everyone and are open to everyone.

It is important to state this at the outset, for there are those Christians in the United Kingdom and the United States who would instinctively wish to dismiss her as another 'trendy lefty', a political maverick who is contaminating the gospel through her political pronouncements. She reminds us that the gospel is about love and justice, or it lapses into mere sentimentality.

Dorothee Soelle sees *us* as those 'who prefer not to decide'. She has a message and a challenge. We put ourselves 'above the conflict'. We temporize with 'eternal indecision'. She reminds us on whose side Jesus stood and she bluntly spells it out: 'Put yourself on the side of the damned of this world.' She lays it on the line with no apologies: '*Christ's viewpoint is extremist because his view is that of the victim.*' Jesus' struggle was to make hopes reality. 'But human kind cannot bear very much reality,' as Eliot reminds us. What is the reality of our situation? Like the Israelites of old, we have got used to living in Egypt and have even superimposed it on the rest of the world. *Choosing Life* means three things:

to be free from our captivity,

to rediscover a sense of discontent

which can take us beyond cynicism and apathy.

Those Christians who dare read this book will learn that faith means that we are capable of changing things and we must not go on defending the system but must struggle to humanize life itself.

Dorothee Soelle's book contains a moving account of some time she spent in Argentina. It is not only in this chapter, but throughout her thinking, that she incarnates her theology in suffering humanity. Her whole object is to fight the destructive forces of cynicism which paralyse much of Western Christianity. She wants to see us free from our captivity to consumerism, which has inevitably led us in the West to 'the looting of the Third World, the destruction of nature, the suppression of the liberation movements and militarization'.

As I write this, two of my closest friends, Dan and Phil Berrigan, are facing from five to ten years imprisonment for actively taking on the principalities and powers of evil in America. They destroyed the nose-cone of a rocket designed to wipe out a whole city, probably in the Soviet Union. They are friends of Dorothee Soelle's, too, and, like her, refuse to accept the possibility of the world being annihilated by atomic bombs and have acted. Dorothee Soelle challenges us to fight against the appalling cynicism that allows Christians to contemplate the mass destruction of God's world. 'Do not let your faith and hope be destroyed. We need one another in order to believe.'

I read *Choosing Life* after suffering a heart attack, the trauma of which can hardly be described. Why do I think this book to be vital if our Christian life and witness is to be revitalized in Britain today? Because this gifted woman has encapsulated that liberation which Jesus proclaimed both in his living and dying. 'The truth will set you free.' The author speaks of the need to be liberated from class, war, materialism, racism, sexism and all the other violences and blindnesses we are prone to. *Choosing Life* is a great book in every sense, because it gives us the incentive to be freed from fear and makes us more capable of love through our commitment to struggle with and for the oppressed. Thus we are moved from our 'living and partly living' situations, from lives of repetitive monotony, through taking up the cause of the oppressed and, by so doing, begin to experience for ourselves the resurrection life his early followers knew.

This life in struggle and suffering is the truth for our life too. Nothing came to an end with Jesus' death. Everything only began, properly speaking. That's resurrection.

Namibia Peace Centre,   Colin O'Brien Winter
London

1 Faith as a Struggle against Objective Cynicism

'The real exile of Israel in Egypt was that they had learned to endure it,' says Rabbi Hanokh in the Hassidim stories which Martin Buber collected.[1] I am talking to you here as someone belonging to the so-called First World of the industrial West. And the real exile of Christians in the First World is that we have learnt to put up with that exile.

We do not look on our life in the affluent society as if we were in Egypt. On the contrary, we have adapted ourselves to it to such an extent that in the very midst of Egypt, under the domination of Pharaoh, we feel quite at home. We Christians in the First World have adapted ourselves to the Egyptian way of life, and we have taken over the Egyptians' fundamental outlook – the assumption, for example, that individualism is the highest stage of human development; or the assumption that history is a senseless seesaw; sometimes one group is up; sometimes – after a revolution, perhaps – it's another. We have learnt very successfully to endure our exile – so successfully that as Christians we no longer see ourselves as being in exile at all, or as strangers in a foreign country. In fact we are more concerned to Egyptianize the whole world. We consider that the countries which have not as yet adapted

themselves completely to the capitalist way of life and its
system of values are 'not yet' as advanced as ourselves.
The context of our lives is Egypt; but we try by all possible
means to avoid taking this historical context of ours seriously. We prefer to ontologize Egypt, saying that the things
we don't approve of in our countries are in accordance
with man's sinful nature, which is an eternally given fact.
We declare that certain quite specific human characteristics, which have without any doubt developed in the course
of history, are simply natural – competitive greed, for example, or envy, and the lust for possession. The Egyptian
way of life seems to us the natural one. We don't remember
that once upon a time there were people who preferred the
desert to our cities, and conflict to our peace; that they
chose hunger instead of the meat we eat – meat produced
from the corn which the hungry lack.

In the First World we have learnt to put up with exile,
and that means that we have even forgotten the thirst for
justice and righteousness. We have become one with the
objective cynicism of the prevailing culture.

When I received the invitation to talk to you here, I
asked myself what I could say to people in Buenos Aires.
I don't believe that the Christian faith is being properly
interpreted if it is reduced to timeless, generalized truths.
Contextuality is the Bible's hermeneutical principle, not
generality. If I want to try to pass on what Christianity
means to me, I don't have to look for some satellite high
up in the sky, from which messages are sent to both Ham-
burg and Buenos Aires. I only have to sink myself deeply
enough in the piece of earth in which I live. My thinking
has to spring from my own context, or I shall simply be an
intellectual manager who fits in everywhere, or a church
bureaucrat without any roots. The truth is not generally
applicable. It is specific and concrete.

I cannot bring you the theology you need. That would

be arrogance and cultural imperialism. What I can do is to try to say as honestly as I can why I, a white woman belonging to the middle classes of the First World, need faith. Why I am afraid of sin. What it means to bear the cross. In what way Christ restores the offended dignity of men and women, and what resurrection means. In all these questions I have learnt a great deal from various Latin American theologians; but the theological attempt I am about to make is not a kind of barter in which Europeans are supposed to supply the general truths of faith, and the Latin Americans are to offer a specific application. What I am attempting is to be a Christian in the context of the rich and despairing world.

I have asked myself what this can offer you and what profit it could be to you to listen to German or North American theology. I have grappled with this question and should like to answer it on two levels: on the sociological plane and on the theological one. Sociologically and politically we can start from the plans of the rulers and from technocratic hopes. The 'undeveloped' are to be 'developed'. The Third World is the world of the 'not yet'. Its future is foreshadowed in the First World and has already been reached there. So when I try to describe the First World, I am making a statement about what at best awaits you, in the framework of the development design. At the same time I am talking to those of you are who closer to us in the First World than most of your fellow-countrymen – to the élite and to all the people who would like to belong to the élite. But I am talking, not as a neutral observer but as a Christian who thinks theologically. I am describing the world in which I live (and in which you are already living to some extent) in terms of particular theological catchwords: Egypt, cynicism, estrangement, death. I am talking about Egypt and about the extremely pleasant life at Pharaoh's court; but it could well be that later on you

3

too will perhaps be in the same danger of forgetting. All our upbringing and education in the First World is directed towards smothering our need for liberation and towards making us forget that need. I don't know whether things are very different in your schools and universities. But perhaps we can rebel against the forgetfulness that is planned for us, reminding one another of the promise given to us:

> If I forget you, O Jerusalem,
> let my right hand wither!
> Let my tongue cleave to the root of my mouth,
> if I do not remember you,
> if I do not set Jerusalem
> above my highest joy (Ps. 137.5f.).

To remember Jerusalem in the midst of Egypt means defining our need for liberation and denouncing the Egypt in which we live. Let me try to do this in the context of the First World.

At the beginning of the 70s, the firm of Levi-Strauss brought out a new advertising slogan for their Jesus jeans which reflects the spirit of the second industrial revolution and the transformation of traditional ideas and values which is involved in it. This new slogan was: 'Thou shalt have no other jeans before me.' The Italian writer and film producer Pier Paolo Pasolini subjected this slogan to a 'linguistic analysis',[2] which discloses something about the mental and spiritual situation of the time. Pasolini sees the emergence of a 'right-wing revolution' which, at the beginning of the 70s, reached Italy as well. This revolution is far-reaching, touches the very substance of life, and is absolutely new, in that it first destroys and then redefines all existing institutions – the family, culture, language and the church. He calls this new state of affairs 'hedonistic fascism' or '*consumismo*'. Consumerism is the perfect and inexorable repression of all 'existential absoluteness'. Belief in the non-derivable meaning of life is no longer presupposed.[3] Consumerism emerged when the era of bread (as Pasolini calls it) ended. This is the most important change in Europe since the Second World War – the most important economic, political and cultural event. Pasolini maintains that historical fascism did not inflict so much as a scratch on the soul of the Italian people, whereas the new consumerism is the perfect suppression of what used to be called the soul.

The Swiss writer Otto F. Walter[4] describes our situation as 'the new fascism which operates anonymously'. Life in Western Europe, he says, is life 'in occupied territory'. Our everyday life, our work, our relationships to one another are controlled by an occupying power, 'this gelatinous, slimy fascism, which penetrates everything'. The occupation has taken place in the midst of the official bourgeois democracies: 'Supermarkets, big banks, major technology, mass-media, cartels, stock exchanges, holdings, monopolies, international financial capital', to take only a few key words. All society's institutions have been taken over by this occupying power. Having once occupied them, they undermine them: the family, schools, the media, parliament, the churches, the courts, the universities, literature, medicine, town planning – all institutions which earlier maintained some degree of independence and tried to guarantee a certain humane quality in life. Of course the actual functioning of these institutions was not without its problems; but, in competition with other powers, they did represent the interests of children, for example, or the sick, or the people living in a certain district. Under the new power they have become the agents of that anonymous power; they serve the values which now control our lives and they are only permitted in so far as they subject themselves to these values. 'Here are a few phrases round which the creed of that power is grouped; growth at any price; profit at any price; competition at any price; the club-law of freedom for business at any price; performance and achievement at any price; discipline; charity; discipline; supervision; controls; limited liability; supervision; discipline; and recreation . . .' The subjection of life to these values is not brought about by violence, as it was in the old, open, militaristic fascism. It is as 'soft' as the TV commercials that mould the consciousness of children in a different way from any educational situation history has hitherto known.

In European theology we have hardly considered the results of this occupation, of this transformation of our whole life. But it is above all our faith, our practice, which has no relation to this new reality. It is so weak, so diverted towards matters of minor importance, that up to now we have still hardly enunciated any Christian answer to this event.

In the age of bread, human life could either find some meaning or it remained without one. The human fears of loss of the self and the senselessness of life found expression in the language of religion. 'Seek first the kingdom of God and all these things (meaning food, drink and clothing) shall be yours as well' (Matt. 6.33). This language of existential absoluteness is based on the assumption that our lives can be a whole. There are situations in which we experience ourselves as unseparated, undivided, with all our capabilities and dimensions, our past and our future. The oil in the lamps of the virgins waiting for the bridegroom is an image of this wholeness. If the oil is missing, everything is missing. They are then 'foolish' – unprepared, scattered and dispersed in a thousand different ways. If their lamps are full of oil, they don't need to worry; they are completely 'on the ball', as we say.

Faith as a Struggle against Objective Cynicism

Existential absoluteness takes shape in the indivisible wholeness for which I make my decision. 'Choose life' presupposes that 'life' in this emphatic and absolute sense really exists, and that we can choose it and lay hold of it, or can throw it away or miss it completely.

> I call heaven and earth to witness against you this day, that I have set before you life and death, blessing and curse; therefore choose life, that you and your descendants may live (Deut. 30.19).

Choosing life in the face of death means chiming in with the great 'Yes' to life. In the biblical context it means living and multiplying – and both of these were threatened in Egypt. It means living in the land, being blessed, having peace.

We are inclined to affirm life under particular circumstances, under certain given conditions – when life is young, and beautiful and full of achievement. The 'Yes' which is meant in the emphatic, biblical sense is a 'Yes' without any conditions. It applies in sickness and dying as well. It applies above all to the people who have felt themselves to be denied and without dignity for so long that they have come to terms with the situation.

But choosing life is the very capacity for *not* putting up with the matter-of-course destruction of life surrounding us, and the matter-of-course cynicism that is our constant companion.

Choosing life is what the Christian tradition calls 'faith', in the existential sense of trust, not in the rational sense of believing something to be true.

> Therefore choose life, that you and your descendants may live, loving Yahweh your God, obeying his voice and cleaving to him; for that means life to you and length of days, that you may dwell in the land which Yahweh

swore to your fathers, to Abraham, to Isaac, and to Jacob, to give them (Deut. 30.19f.).

A language was developed within this tradition which reminds us of this very emphasis on life, its endangering and the rescue of it – a language that makes life in this sense present to us and so makes it possible.

The awareness that life is at stake, and that it can become meaningless, has found expression in the religious traditions. There people's fears of losing themselves and losing life's meaning were put into words. Of course these fears could be manipulated. 'Save us from hell' was a prayer that ran through the ages. This was an expression of something which to experience at all today means being in a fit state for the psychiatric hospital: fear of missing life, fear of the destruction of the whole, fear of being lost. In the midst of life we do not live, in the midst of permanently heated rooms the cold creeps in upon us. 'Everything's quite dead' is a favourite answer one hears from young people if one asks what is going on here or there.

It is possible to miss the whole of life, to throw it away, to treat it as a disposable object. We can lose it or gain it; we don't, at all events, 'possess' it. But we have no language which is expressive and transcending enough for us to talk to each other about this. Yet without this existential fear for life, there is no deeper love for life either. There is only the prevailing superficial, permanently frustrated and easily aggressive mood which can at any time suddenly switch over into a diffused sadness. Objective cynicism exists in what determines the structure of our lives – the economic looting of the Third World, the destruction of nature, the suppression of liberation movements. This economic and political structure of rule is secured by a growing militarization of society. Twenty years ago the remilitarizing of Western Germany, after two lost world wars, was a passionately contested subject; today it is a matter of course. People talk about the victims of political terrorism, but the far greater number of victims claimed by a completely normal military manoeuvre in the autumn of 1977 get only a passing mention. The fears of the population are directed away from the real threats to minor conflicts. In the United States today the work of 51 out of every 100 scientists has something to do with rearmament. These people are planning, experimenting, researching in the interests of a greater capacity for killing. When the readiness for overkill is one of society's essential goals, the everyday consciousness of the individual does not remain uninfluenced either by society's general structure.

In a society that is orientated towards suppression and death, in which consumerism has taken the place of the older religions of rural Catholicism and middle-class Protestantism, the individual too is caught up in society's objective cynicism. New and widely diffused neuroses are springing up in mass numbers; identity crises, lack of motivation, depressions and profound self-doubt are no longer the luxury problems of the upper middle classes. They are now affecting apprentices, students, the young unemployed. Relations between people are breaking up, and the pauperization of the masses which Marx prophesied has come about, not – as he assumed it would – in material terms but in psychological ones. Life is involved in a legitimation crisis. For an increasing number of people, meaning and trust in the whole have come to be out of reach. Something is lacking – something which the existential philosophy of the 30s called 'existential absoluteness' – an affirmation of the whole, a kind of love for life. This existential absoluteness has two aspects: an integrative aspect – the being-whole – and a voluntative one – the decision for life. When in biblical language we say 'choose life', these two aspects of integration and decision are the premises. Without them it is impossible to understand love of life in its deeper sense.

We can only love something which is threatened, endangered, something which could be different from what it is, or which could fail to exist altogether. That is to say, we cannot love something that is dead. Existential absoluteness goes with existential anxiety; the emphatic interpretation of life as further growth, as being touched and touching, as developing to new quality and different experiences – this qualitative understanding of life contains within itself an emphatic and traumatic relationship to death. We are killable. To know that is more important than to repeat that we are mortal. Perhaps no one knows that as well as the mentally sick. Life can be lost on the way to being born and before we die. If it were otherwise, life could not be won either.

But it is just this which is extinguished in the thoughtless triviality of the blasphemy 'Thou shalt have no other jeans before me'. Inherent in this slogan is 'the spirit of the second industrial revolution and the mutation of values that is bound up with it'.[5] The circulation of production and consumption moves most smoothly when people are cut off from the experience of nature and history – that is to say, in a world given over to technology, a world that is totally worldly and free of religion.

It is as if all experience of history has disappeared, and above all the history that was read with the eyes of the hopeless. Its point of reference, the kingdom of God and his new righteousness, has become inconceivable; the cyclical interpretation of history has overpowered the interpretation that is eschatologically directed towards a goal.

Disappearance of continuity and calculated lack of memory are necessary for hedonistic consumerism, because having a memory involves an attitude that is hostile to the consumer society. Lack of history is at the same time absence of future and is in this sense undramatic hopelessness. 'Happy Days' à la Beckett are ahead of us, everyone is buried in sand, sitting in his hole, incapable of movement, babbling away and waiting for dawn and sunset with a complete absence of emphasis.

It is not the advertising slogan that makes use of the first commandment which is blasphemy; it is all advertisements. Every attempt to direct the interests of my life towards hair spray, cat food and trips to Ibiza is an attack on the One in whose image I am made.

Consumerism means that my eyes will be incessantly insulted, my ears will be closed, my hands will be robbed of their creativity. My relationships to other people are subject to laws which earlier generations never dreamt of. If everything is experienced and measured in terms of 'having', there is no time and no strength and no language left for being-together.

Faith means fighting against the prevailing cynicism and standing up to it.

In order to understand what the Christian tradition means by faith, we must talk about the alternative to faith. What is it that dominates people when they are lacking in faith. Who or what contests our faith? The evangelists put faith on the one side and fear on the other. The disciples who were in danger of shipwreck while Jesus was asleep in the ship are rebuked: 'Why are you afraid? Have you no faith?' (Mark 4.40). 'Do not fear. Only believe', says Jesus to Jairus, whose daughter is dead (Mark 3.36). Fear of particular threatening events – specific fears – puts us in a state of suspension in which our powers are not concentrated; but so does the fear of life's routine meaninglessness. Everything which we cannot back up with all our faith is evil and cuts us off from that wholeness and unity of life which we call God. As Paul says in his letter to the Romans,

'Whatever does not proceed from faith is sin' (Rom. 14.23). That isn't a moral judgment – it's a theological one.

Take for example a little bank clerk who uses her computer to look after other people's savings books, debts and securities. What Mary does, doesn't 'proceed from faith', not out of certainty, not out of a wholeness. The apparatus of financial capital has power over her, a power that is seemingly neutral. The political part played by the bank, which finances particular economic projects, doesn't interest her. She doesn't know anything about what finance means for society. Perhaps Mary guesses that what she does in the bank is neither a blessing for her fellow men and women, nor is it in their interests. But she has no alternative. Is this sin, then, as Paul asserts in such radical terms? Isn't what she does really neutral? If one learns to think theologically, one realizes that there is no neutrality in this sense. Either Mary can work for the good of society with what she does – that is to say, she can affirm her work and consider it to be useful – or she has to live in a state which I have called objective cynicism. She may quite well at the same time be a nice, decent girl who is anything but cynical. But she and most other people in the First World live in a situation which is objectively cynical. Nothing that she does in her work 'proceeds from faith'; this job has nothing to do with her life as a whole, and with its practice. So faith is moved out into the sphere of recreation and private life. The lower-middle-class virtue of decency has then to do duty for lack of faith. Most of the unimportant Nazis in Germany were always quite decent; that is to say, they were personally honest in the midst of a criminal situation. But what can Mary do except fill up the cheques decently, avoid annoying her boss and treat the customers politely? Can you have faith at all in an objectively cynical situation? You are certain that what you spend all your time doing has no influence. The work has no aim beyond the wages it brings. Your interests go no further than survival. Life is treated like a disposable object – simply something to be thrown away.

But faith – not being afraid – means having a deeper trust in life than the one that surrounds us and to which we have been trained up. The world in which I live represents a whole structure of interpretations which for me are foregiven; every child knows that cars are more important than children – that they need more room and more looking after; every young person knows that profit-bringing rationalization is more important than the preservation of jobs. Every young teacher knows that a school or class that functions well, without any conflicts, is more important for the bureaucracy above her than the children entrusted to her and their needs. The simple facts of our lives reflect the interpretations which indicate that people are objectively unimportant, replaceable and a hindrance. They present themselves as the dominating framework of objective cynicism. If in the United States 48 cents out of every dollar in taxation goes into the production of death, then objective cynicism is embedded in this whole interpretation of life, in the macro-sociology. How can we counter it?

The objective presupposition of a life that is built up economically on exploitation and militarily on terror fundamentally contradicts faith, fearlessness and trust in life. Our experience of impotence makes us dependent and conditions us. And yet according to what the Bible tells us we have to be able to talk about the unconditional nature of faith: fear not – only believe. The Bible is realistic enough to be aware of our fear, but it still reckons with our capacity for believing. You can trust, you can rely on the interpretation of life as good, in spite of objective cynicism, and in the very face of it. Contrary to objective cynicism and contrary to calculated hopelessness (for example, the calculated millions of unemployed and unemployable, as the cynical word designates them), the Christian tradition says; only believe, only trust! Fight against objective cynicism and see to it that it does not settle down subjectively in your heart. Do not allow your faith and hope to be destroyed. Let yourself in for the venture of interpreting life as good: for there have been people who have escaped from Egypt.

If I tell someone in a particular situation, believe! that is not just a moral demand like 'Don't break bottles on the beach!' It is more than that, because when I am talking to a person who believes very little, or not at all, I bring faith with me, or awaken it in the other person. I share the faith and courage, I expand the other person's area of freedom. I alter his previous interpretation of other people and himself. We need one another in order to be able to believe, and in order to be able to fight against objective cynicism. Recruitment for faith has itself a transcending, changing power. The language of faith equips us for the struggle against the objective cynicism of our situation. It does not merely repeat what was; it does not merely reflect what is; it opens and changes. We learn to understand our lives as a struggle against the prevailing cynicism. We understand ourselves in unity with Christ as a part of the kingdom-of-God movement for righteousness. We will be involved in conflicts. It is no longer enough to be personally decent and inoffensive. It never was enough, incidentally.

The language which expresses and evokes the struggle against objective cynicism is changing, transcending, real language, in which we do not inform ourselves about something other than ourselves, but in which we share our own life, our struggle and our pain with one another. Because of its transforming character, which transcends what actually exists, this language of the Christian community is also called the word of God. This is not the word which is preserved in a certain book or which is assigned to a certain institution or its office-bearers. It is the word that quickens us, that allows us to choose life. It is a word that liberates us, so that we know that we are not subject to the commandment 'Thou shalt have no other jeans before me', and that we can overcome this world.

What is faith? 'Faith is the assurance of things hoped for, the conviction of things not seen' (Heb. 11.1). This confidence, this trust is nothing other than our choice for life. It is a great 'Yes' to life, even if life itself is denied in the objective cynical situation. If we are capable of choice, this also presupposes our power to struggle.

In January 1976 I was standing in front of the Pentagon with a little group of Catholic resistance fighters belonging to the Berrigan brothers' group. We were demonstrating against rearmament in a symbolic action. 'Disarm or dig graves' was our slogan, and some of us, reckoning with arrest, dug a grave and put a man into it, wrapped in an American flag. A second group tried to negotiate with the appropriate senator, and a third group – to which I belonged – knelt in the bitter cold in front of the building in which all the power of this world seemed to be gathered together. We sang and prayed. A car containing Pentagon officials drove slowly along our ranks. One of us called out to the driver 'Choose life!' and the gentleman in the grey suit answered, clearly and distinctly, 'No!' I haven't heard the prevailing 'No' as distinctly as that for a long time.

Faith is the struggle against objective and subjective cynicism. The question for Christians in the First World is: do we want to choose life, or the death that has been prepared for us in a hundred different ways? Are we capable at all of going beyond the objective cynicism of the given situation? Faith is practice, is acting – strugglingly and sufferingly – in the interest of the life that is invisible.

How do we arrive at the great 'Yes'? How do we become capable of fighting against cynicism? How is the militancy of life achievable?

The theological tradition answers this question by pointing to grace. The turning away from objective cynicism, the turning to life is not something I can perform or achieve. It is the life that has been damaged or destroyed or cut short which calls me; it is God himself, who calls me to repentance.

To arrive at faith, and to arrive at faith once more, and to overcome the cynicism in me, the agent of capitalism, is an experience of happiness. Once I have given my assent to the great 'Yes', when I have become practised in the struggle against cynicism, when I have resolved to choose life, then I find that I am not the lord who disposes over my own 'Yes'. We are not simply the masters of our faith. The 'Yes', like every real 'Yes', is always an answering, a responsive 'Yes'. The responsive character belongs to the experience of happiness in general. Happiness is not simply being able to speak; it is rather cor*respond*ence – the correspondence with some other person or some other situation. It means letting oneself be touched, and taking sides, although the cynicism of our situation is just that it makes us incapable of suffering or of compassion. The objective cynicism of the situation, economically and politically secured as it is, finds psychological expression in the fantastic techniques for avoiding suffering. To avoid suffering has advanced to the position of a major strategy in the consumer culture, whether physically by means of pills, psychologically by means of diversion, or politically through blindness. We have developed techniques of all kinds in order to avoid suffering, but what we are really avoiding is life itself.

Christ made loving the other person the highest value; but that cannot be done without suffering. When the avoidance of suffering (which means the attempt to get through smoothly and without conflict) is promoted to the rank of highest value then love becomes something subsidiary. In the First World we enjoy a state of injustice as permanent structure, and this has its effects on our system of values. And in this new system of values we have made love and suffering change places, in order of importance. To be free of suffering and to remain so, even when we are dying, is generally recognized as the highest value. Health is the greatest blessing, the bourgeois maxim tells us. To be alive, to transcend our ego and to be in communication and sympathy with everything that lives is subordinated to freedom from suffering. Apathetic freedom from suffering, from privation, from pain, and from involvement has advanced to the position of highest value, like the unwrinkled beauty, the spotless cleanliness and the uninterrupted career which are the characteristics of our way of life compared with that of other nations. The goal of being capable of love and making justice and righteousness possible is subordinated to the other consumerist goal of getting along 'well', which means without damage to ourselves. Instead of getting involved in the struggle against the objective cynicism of our situation, we avoid it. Preventing, avoiding, pushing away, getting out of the way are becoming the essential activities of life.

Faith has a militant element, an element of consciously chosen struggle. Faith in Christ isn't tolerant; it is militant. It has a passionate and unbroken interest in life. It is not reserved and detached. The Bible is certainly full of shy and reticent people who are given a task which they find by nature difficult, but this very shyness and confusion acquire a share in the militancy of faith. The book of Isaiah says about the coming Messiah:

Righteousness shall be the girdle of his waist,

and faithfulness the girdle of his loins (Isa. 11.5).

And we find a similar picture of militancy, of fighting faith, in the letter to the Ephesians:

> Above all take the shield of faith, with which you can quench all the flaming darts of the evil one. And take the helmet of salvation, and the sword of the Spirit, which is the word of God (Eph. 6.16f.).

A degree of steadfastness belongs to the militancy of faith, an unswerving certainty that we are right when we demand more righteousness than we have at present. We are in harmony with the best traditions of mankind when we fight for peace. We have no need to be ashamed of ourselves or to feel small, but can freely acknowledge the militancy of faith. It is the outward side of its beauty.

It is faith that makes people lovely. The person is lovely who does something wholly, without deviation and with all his might. This principle is in accordance with classical aesthetics, in which only that which proceeds from our united powers is called 'beautiful'. Everything that is singular, isolated, is to be condemned, as Goethe says. Every example of isolation of an individual human potentiality, every over-development of one power at the cost of the others is 'singularity'. The singularity of our rational powers means that we have to suppress or deny our physical and emotional nature. Every expression of life, for example every human relationship, every creative activity, should be 'whole' – that is to say, all our powers should be involved in it. The more of myself I have to deny, repress and stifle in a relationship, the more partial, limited and impoverished the relationship will be. One-dimensionality is the expression of this prevailing impoverishment and destruction. It can reach a particular perfection, but it is lacking in the beauty that comes from the fusing together of all our powers, experiences and relationships.

A person becomes lovely in the experience of the wholeness of his powers, in their unsuppressed co-ordination. 'Faith' is an old religious way of expressing this successful achievement, this wholeness. In faith we are wholly related to the realization of truth, without the exclusion and denial of some of our capabilities. Arriving at faith means entering into the struggle against the prevailing cynicism. It means being more and more free of fear. It means affirming the great 'Yes'. It means renewing and making true the old confidence which perhaps shone into our childhood. It means loving God with all our hearts and all our souls and all our minds, without any reservation, without saying, 'Yes, if you give me this and that', and without saying, 'But you once . . .' It is a 'Yes' without ifs and buts. It is the great 'Yes'. It has a share in the beauty and militancy of life and it is this which makes the lovely what they are, and the militant brave and self-forgetful.

If faith enters a person's heart it is like a betrothal. It is the point in time when subjective cynicism – what I have called the agent of capitalism in our hearts – disappears. According to the prophet Hosea, God tells us:

> I will betroth you to me for ever; I will betroth you to me in righteousness and in justice, in steadfast love, and in mercy. I will betroth you to me in faithfulness; and you shall know the Lord (Hos 2.19f.).

If we take up this language of betrothal, of promise, of involvement, we can say: 'I betroth myself to real life. I will give my life for righteousness and justice. I have chosen life, even if the obvious choice seemed death, and even though the death-wish is strong in me. I am learning the self-surrender of my life.'

2 Sin and Estrangement

Talking about faith means beginning with one's own situation. I am trying to start from the objective cynicism of the Western world. Theological reflection is a second step which follows the analysis of the reality. The first thing – the thing we begin with – is not revelation, or the Bible, or the tradition of the church. It is our own situation, its cynicism and its estrangement. But to grasp a situation properly and to describe it justly always means describing it in its contradictions. It means recognizing what goes beyond the given situation, what the continuing impetus of that situation is. The hermeneutics that begin below, with real people and in a given social situation, do not simply take a photograph of what already exists. In paying attention to the contradictions, we put our ear to the ground and listen to the hope that still calls to us from below the asphalt of our cities. We do not content ourselves with the cynicism. We listen to the signals of the struggle against cynicism. In this sense some theological reflection is already present even in the first step of our hermeneutics, something that has not been destroyed.

In this lecture I want to talk about the estrangement of men and women from themselves, from one another, and from nature. This too is an analysis of reality, an attempt to describe the situation. But in using the word *sin* for this estrangement – not, as it might be, 'the fate of the individual in the industrial era' or 'the price of progress that unfortunately has to be paid', but just this old-fashioned word 'sin' – the first step in the contradiction becomes clear, the suffering over the situation that drives us forward, the element of faith which gives up nothing and nobody. A second step methodologically is then an explicit theological reflection; and here tradition finds its voice. Was it always like this? tradition asks us. How used sin to be interpreted? Did people in earlier times deal with sin in just the same way as we do? Or differently? And what can this teach us? The third step which we ought then to take would be the practical perspectives, the strategies of reconciliation. These three steps can also be formally termed the 'practice – theory – practice' model: believe, reflect, and then believe again in a new and better way.

Let me begin with a poem by the English psychiatrist R. D. Laing.[1] It is a kind of poetical riddle, but the author is not aiming to put us in a position to solve the riddle. The idea is rather that we should learn *how* to solve it, and how to seek the answers.

> never saw it
> never heard it
> never smelt it, touched it
>   or tasted it
> never felt it
> never heard it mentioned
>
> never had any idea of it
> never dreamt of it
> never wanted it
> never missed it
>   is there a problem?

What is this 'it', which is never seen, heard, felt or wanted?

What word would you put in? Perhaps the soul which you have never felt? Perhaps life – never had any idea of it? Perhaps the Holy Spirit – never dreamt of it? But the point of this little poem is not to solve the riddle. The point is to describe the mass phenomenon in which people do not even miss life, a desolate, destructive culture in which more and more people are giving up living altogether in the emphatic sense to which the religions of earlier civilizations gave expression. Sin is an expression of being cut off from life, of universal disorder. Sin is a general social climate in which person is the enemy of person and is necessarily understood as being just that. It is the 'guns, not butter' climate, if we are describing the goals of production; it is the climate of competition instead of mutual help, if we are describing the situation in education. I am talking about sin in the singular, the sin sometimes called original sin. I mean the predominant compulsion to sin in a particular society, which is the singular fact on which the plural of many individual sins rests.

It is 'the law of sin and death' (Rom. 8.2) under which we live. When Paul talks about 'the law' he means what we call the economic structure, or the political and economic system: factual compulsions which are neither made nor desired by the individual, but which confront us without our having sought them out. But we affirm them simply by living in them. We submit to superior force; we have to accept economic and technological necessity and the exigencies of the energy policy. In German the word *Sachzwang* – the pressure of circumstances – has come to be used more and more in the last ten years. All the government measures which are against the interests of the local population – for example road and transport planning, or the destruction of the environment – are justified by the words 'pressure of circumstances'. The pressure of technological circumstances is given authority; it can only be criticized by experts, just as the law – as a word used in a religious context – could only be interpreted by rabbis. Perhaps 'pressure of circumstances' is the best translation we could take today for what Paul calls 'the law'.

Let me now offer you an interpretation[2] of some verses of the apostle Paul which clarify the concept of sin:

> Let not sin therefore reign in your mortal bodies, to make you obey their passions. Do not yield your members to sin as instruments of wickedness, but yield yourselves to God as men who have been brought from death to life, and your members to God as instruments of righteousness. For sin will have no dominion over you, since you are not under law but under grace.

The passage is in Romans 6. 12–14. Its context is that the Christian has 'died' through baptism (vv. 2,4,7), that our 'old self' has been 'crucified with him' (v. 6), that we have been 'freed' (v. 7) from the rule of sin, that we are dead to sin but 'alive to God' (v. 11).

I should like to take three steps in this interpretation. First I will try to say what my concern with the text is, and to formulate my questions to it. Then I will try to understand what the text is saying. Finally I will 'translate' the text, paraphrasing and interpreting it, appropriating it, so that its sharpness and immediacy makes itself felt again for us too.

What interests me first of all are the anthropological statements that Paul makes. I have difficulty with expressions like 'mortal body', 'passions', 'members' as 'instruments' or 'weapons'. What assumptions lie behind these words? Can we share them? What does liberation mean for Paul? And in this connection: is what we have been accustomed to call 'redemption' an essentially idealistic term, which also suggests redemption, or deliverance, *from* chains and fetters, from the earthly reality? Redemption or deliverance as a metaphor means the freeing from sickness, captivity, a bad state of affairs, and the transference to another, better one. But is this what Paul is talking about? Is it a part of that dichotomic tradition – the division between spirit and flesh – which in the history of Christendom has promoted and glorified suppression? This dichotomy has its ideological share in sexism, racism and class rule. It was and is an instrument of power, of the will to rule, and in this sense it is imperialistic. In the dichotomic system of thought, people can only be redeemed, transferred to something else, snatched out of the situation they are in. But don't our deepest expectations about life, ourselves and the world go much further? Don't we need more than redemption? Don't we need liberation? What does Paul really mean by *soteria*, salvation? Isn't liberation the best translation, because it includes body and sociality, i.e., what we mean anthropologically and sociologically by the word 'earth'?

But let us go back to the text. Paul seems to me to be saying three things here:

1. To live in a mortal body or, more correctly, to *be* body, means *being dependent*. Paul uses the expressions 'body', 'members', 'instruments' and 'yourselves' parallel to one another. They do not mean component parts of the human organism; they mean existence as a whole. Existence means bodily existence, means being bound, being conditioned, being unfree. 'And because a man's a man he needs something to eat, if you please', as Brecht says. But more than this kind of dependency is meant. We are not merely dependent on biology. We are dependent on our particular rulers at any given time, on their culture, their ideas and laws. My incapacity to accept myself as woman, for example the shame of menstruation, the attempt to deny a dimension of my physical existence, shows me how dominated, how bound, how unfree I am. 'Our physical

nature' says Käsemann on this passage, 'is our condition in a world for which different forces contend and in whose conflict each individual is caught up, belonging to one lord or the other and representing this lord both actively and passively.'[3] In the shame to which I have been trained up by a process of education, in the fears I have internalized, I represent the order which man has established and which is the enemy of creation. I am dependent on the prevailing ideas. I am dependent down to my very dreams. Even my wishes are remote-controlled and destroy me because they function as the instruments of injustice and exploitation. Let me give an example of what I mean. In Latin America in recent years, more and more arable and grazing land has fallen into the hands of foreign companies who use it for luxury export goods. Strawberries are planted, for example, and orchids are cultivated where beans and maize once grew or could grow. 'Do not yield your members to sin as instruments of wickedness.' My consumer desires – perhaps to eat strawberries out of season – function objectively as the instruments of wickedness. The state of the economy on which I am dependent can very easily be related to the mythological images used by Paul about the power of sin which springs into life, seizes power and rules. Within a closed economic system which does not work for the benefit of human needs but for the profits of the possessors, sin – which is to say this system of injustice – has demonic features; it is uncontrollable, we do not understand it, we deny the unjust system and our share in it, and it is all-powerful in a double sense: outwardly, where production is concerned, and inwardly as regards our 'passions'. Late capitalism's main achievement has been the way it has manipulated the desires, the wishes and the dreams of men and women in such a way that they are subjected to the lordship of capital.

2. The second thing that Paul says is that life cannot be

neutral. When we put our abilities, our potentialities, our vital energies (or so I understand the metaphor 'members' which Paul uses) and our whole selves at the disposal of the prevailing injustice, we were already dead. Sin, which is to say injustice, was the king who ruled over us; through our bodies, through our participation in this world, through our conscious or unconscious support for this world. It is impossible to be neutral, because we are always 'in the mode of belongingness and participation',[4] because we are body, relational beings, connected with one another. To be bodily in nature means that 'nobody, fundamentally speaking, belongs to himself alone'.[5] The fact that we 'are made of earth' brings another question in its train: to whom does the earth belong? This is not a fortuitous question, or a merely economic one. The recognition of the material fact that we are made of earth leads directly to the question, to whom, then, the earth belongs. If we were spiritual beings this question about lordship over the earth could be seen as an unnecessary one, because it would be merely wordly or external.

Christoph Blumhardt, a Protestant pastor who became a Social Democrat member of parliament for Württemburg, and one of the fathers of the present-day 'Christians for Socialism' movement, wrote in the 1890s:

> We should not ask subjectively: Shall I be justified before God? We should ask . . .: How does God's righteousness come upon me? Objectively . . . the Bible never talks about 'being reckoned righteous before God'. Luther only translated the phrase like that because he had the wrong idea in mind. Then the Bible had to give way. But what is written in the Bible is always 'the righteousness, of God', and this comes through faith, not through the law.[6]

The dispute is an old one. The righteousness that is

26

reckoned before God, and which is promised to me as someone who is outside it, is a basic experience affecting the subject. It is the transition from despair to practice. The fact that there is no neutrality in life means that there is nothing between despair/sin on the one hand and practice/faith on the other. There is no other more peaceful, more harmless alternative. The expression 'righteousness that counts before God' reflects this in relation to the person. But God's righteousness means more than this transition. It affects the material body and the earth, which belong together. The earth stops being a place where life is rejected, a place of exploitation, a place of injustice. In the bourgeois Protestant eras, God's righteousness was interpreted in the sense of a profound personalism. A contemporary materialist interpretation means that the earth becomes God's earth. How? Blumhardt also wrote, on New Year's Eve, 1911:

> In earlier decades, at the time when I was born, there was a terrible famine, a want of daily bread, so that people often did not know where to turn. It is a thing of the past. I reckon everything that is happening in our own time in relation to what is to come. 'He is coming with the clouds' – that is to say, not just to you, or to me, or to us, or to this or that community or group: he will appear to people everywhere according to God's decree and will, and in a way entirely his own, quite materially – in the way that electric light has begun to light up our stables and cowsheds. He is coming in the whole development of the age.

Blumhardt interprets 'God comes' quite materially. By doing so he of course lays himself open to attack in a very different way from an idealistic interpretation that talks neither about famine nor about electric light. To lay oneself open to attack is one dimension of what it means to remain true to the earth. It is the reason which makes Paul, in another passage, call the community of Christians 'fools for Christ's sake' (I Cor. 4.10).

3. Paul's third statement contradicts traditional Protestant thinking even more than the others. For this thinking is essentially determined by an anthropological pessimism which expects everything bad of people and nothing good and which, especially, doesn't expect anything of Christ either. Paul says in this text that in Christ *we are capable of righteousness*. We can put our members – i.e., our capabilities, our potentialities, our vital energies – at life's disposal. We can make ourselves the weapons of righteousness, the instruments of peace whom God uses. It is not true that, whether we are Christians or not, we are at the mercy of the forces of circumstance which dominate us. For we are not subject to the laws of the imperialistic structure of exploitation; we are subject to grace. Faith means that we do not have to go on living as hitherto, subject to iron compulsions. We can exchange our dependency for a new, freely accepted faithfulness to the earth.

Paul puts this fundamental conversion down to grace. It is grace to arrive at practice from despair, and dependency on those who rule us. It is grace to live in resistance. It is grace to work for liberation.

Our bodies and our lives then exist for the sake of righteousness, not in an idealistic sense, but in a practical and material one. Justification and sanctification coincide. This is most clearly visible in the word *paristanein*, which one can translate as 'giving oneself' to God (with the erotic connotations of the phrase) or, in a military sense, as 'seconded for God's service'. It means to be ready for service, to put oneself at someone's disposal or to make oneself available – to be *disponible* as the French worker priests put it, to enter into an obligation, a commitment which changes my body, my real life. The place where I live will look different. The time I take for certain things alters. My priorities can no longer be part of this world – that is to say, they can no longer revolve round money and 'consumption'. To be in Christ means completing the great self-surrender. The Taizé Easter message for 1970 said: 'The risen Christ will prepare us to give our lives, so that person is no longer the victim of person.' To give one's life, to yield oneself up, is an expression that can be used for martyrdom – I am thinking of Elisabeth Käsemann, for example, who gave her life so that person should no longer be the victim of person. But this surrender begins at an earlier point. It also has the sense of the daily surrender of the body, reality, money, professional security. The fact that sin will have no power over us means the surrender of my life to the point of no return. This point, says Paul, can be reached. Let me paraphrase the text again:

> The system of injustice shall therefore no longer determine the way you live, so that you run after false dreams. Do not put your capabilities at the service of capital; it uses them as a weapon for exploitation. But give yourself to God, as those who having once been without ability to communicate and without power have now come alive. Put your potentialities and capabilities at the service of life, as a weapon for justice and righteousness. For the system of injustice will not be able to break you, since you are subject, not to the force of circumstances, but to grace.

This force of circumstances, this law, separates us from God, estranges us from a life that could be termed human. Estrangement, alienation, is a term which Hegel took over from the Christian tradition and to which he gave new content. 'Love reconciles life to itself', says Hegel. He gives the name estrangement to the phase of non-reconciliation, self-emptying, separation and pain too. It is a necessary transition on the way to reconciliation.

In a famous chapter in his *Phenomenology of Mind*, Hegel related this concept of necessary estrangement to the most important modern life-process: work. In the chapter on master and servant, Hegel sets up a new theory about human labour. He distinguishes two forms of human existence. In the one a person is so bound to his work that it determines his whole life; whereas in the other form of living, a man takes possession of another person's labour and possesses it. The former, the servant, is completely at the mercy of his master, for the master possesses the means of reproducing life. This dependency of the one on the other is not founded on weakness or natural inferiority – the servant is not lazier or stupider or 'less developed' than his master; it is rather created by the fact of possession. The servant, the slave, the wage-earner becomes a thing whose existence consists of simply being used. It is just this that Hegel calls a person's estrangement or alienation, because that human being has then lost his humanity; for his humanity consists in his being an end in himself and not a means to something else. If this humanity is lost in the realm of work, the loss cannot be compensated for elsewhere, in a person's free time, for example. It is a widespread illusion that a human being can still be a person in at least one section of life, even if this humanity is denied him in all other essential sectors. It is an error frequently reiterated by bourgeois sociology that freedom, adventure, self-determination and happiness can be salvaged for the private sphere, since they are unobtainable in public and working life. The burden which then falls on the intimate sphere, in the midst of a life which is in general wrong, destroys the intimate sphere itself.

Hegel at least is far removed from a compensation ideology of this kind, which itself defines work as de-humanizing. Hegel's analysis also brings about the dialectical reversal into liberation through work. In Hegel's view, the lord or master lives from the productivity of his servants. He himself is not productive and active. He is not involved. This idleness belongs to the very nature of the situation and is dangerous for the master himself. He has robbed himself of the means of human self-realization; he doesn't learn anything any more; he has no new experiences; whereas, on the other hand, the process of work itself alters the consciousness of the worker. Hegel believes that the labourer, the servant, the one who is weak, is stronger than his master, because he works. The person who possesses nothing except the hands he works with becomes stronger by having contact with the earth, by being a mediator with nature, as Hegel puts it. Historically it can be said that the labourer or servant represents the progressive forces of history. He is exploited and alienated, but he works; he goes on producing; he empties himself into his work; he alienates himself but he wins himself back. The need to produce something makes it possible for him to realize himself at the same time. That is not abstract philosophy. I think that everyone who has ever worked creatively knows this dialectic of work. There is alienation, boredom, determination by someone or something outside oneself, a going out of oneself into what is extraneous and strange; and there is also the other experience of finding oneself again in productive work. Work is part of our self-realization. The person who loses himself finds himself. The emptying of oneself, the alienation, is a necessary step on the road to the birth of men and women as human beings. There is no direct way into unalienated life, indeed this wish, which we all cherish, is a childish one.

We have to leave paradise, we have to discover the alien world of objects, if we are to be able to return into a then altered world.

In Hegel's thinking, alienation or estrangement has a double meaning. On the one hand it is dependency, exploitation, loss of the self; yet at the same time the concept has its own dialectic, which is conceived entirely in the framework of the Jewish-Christian tradition. To talk about the worker's estrangement means talking about the strength of the weak, about the courage of those who have been denied their rights, about the truth of the people who are hungry, about the liberation of the dependent. In theology people like to talk in generally highly abstract terms about hope. For me, the decisive thing seems to be towards whom the hope is directed, and who lives from hope. Tradition answers: it is the poor, 'servants', to use Hegel's term. Hope exists for them, not as something which one can have or not have, as often seems the case to a middle-class person, but as something vitally necessary. The only way in which middle-class people can participate in hope is if they make the hopes of the oppressed their own and share in them.

But let us go back to Hegel's idea: the idea that people's estrangement from themselves through work also liberates them again and leads them home. Is this not all too idealistic an assumption – the assumption that through their work workers could gain the strength of the weak? Does Hegel's thinking here not belong to a pre-industrial context, in which even the dependent shoemaker's journeyman could enjoy the experience of productivity? Isn't the new experience, compared with this, precisely that people can no longer realize themselves in their work, because they are estranged and divided from every relevant element of productivity? Workers do not plan what they produce. In the chemical industry, for example, they are not asked whether they would prefer to make plastic into napalm bombs, or into toys. Moreover they are estranged from the process of organizing labour, which contributes to creativity; they have no way of co-determining the organization of work, the way the time is divided up, the speed at which it is done and the division of labour. They are a part of the process, but are without any power or control over that process. The sale and distribution of the things they have produced are out of their control as well. It is the all-powerful 'free market' which demands, for example, that foodstuffs should be destroyed rather than sold cheaply. The whole idea of throw-away production is in itself an attack on the value and creativity of human labour. If what I have made is just good enough to disappear into the dustbin before it is used at all, what does this fact have to say about me? What will happen to me when I am old?

The workers are also cut off from the added value of what they produce, and not only because the wage they are paid is often too little, even in the wealthy countries. The estrangement of people through paid labour would continue even if the wages were higher, as long as the added value produced in common were still taken possession of individually and not collectively. Our great and essential needs are collective; we share them with others: the need for water and air, for transport and communications, for education and health, for a share in cultural and political activities and the power to co-determine them. But the state of self-estrangement in the system of paid labour prevents these needs of ours from being fulfilled. The very thing which in Hegel's analysis expressed the hope for liberation – that the workers themselves realize themselves in their work, that they win back their self-emptied lives – is the very thing that is still denied to us under the economic conditions that are based on private property and whose goal is accordingly not the satisfaction of needs but the increase of profit. The self-alienation of workers remains, even in rich industrial nations. The fundamental social contradictions between capital and labour remain – the contrast, for example between production of foodstuffs in the interests of men and women and their health, and the production of foodstuffs deleterious to health in the interests of profit. Basic economic contradictions are the conditions for what I have called the objective cynicism of the situation, with its trend towards self-destruction. The objective contempt with which I am treated in my work prepares the ground for the mental and psychological misery existing in the highly industrialized countries, which shows itself in mass alcoholism, in the suicide statistics, and in mental disturbances.

We can follow the classic philosophical tradition and, like Karl Marx, distinguish between four different forms of alienation or estrangement among working people. They are estranged from nature, from themselves, from their fellows, and from their species. To be estranged from nature means denying the deep significance of human labour, which lies in the reconciliation between nature and mankind. It means looking on nature as an exploitable object and treating it as such. Our deepest experience in work has to do with the encounter with nature, but the industrial and office worker is excluded from this give and take, from true creative dealings with creation. A short while ago I saw a poster which showed a photograph of part of the globe, taken from the air. The earth was torn and full of craters. The caption was: Love your mother.

Estrangement or sin means a structure that is imposed on us; living under it we cannot do what is good. Sin means being compelled to sin, being trained to destroy, being brought up to plunder. Following the law of our world we cannot 'love our mother'. As long as we are not in Christ but are under the law, under the lordship of the industrial culture stamped by capitalism, estrangement rules over us and our whole relationship to creation is disturbed.

Secondly, the worker is estranged from himself. Many

different phenomena demonstrate this. Let me pick out one: the relationship of the worker to time. Most of those involved have no say in the way work is organized and assigned. They have to adapt themselves to the rhythm of the machine or the conveyer belt. And this means that for the factory worker time disintegrates. It becomes a not-time – indeed the very feeling for time dies. Simone Weil has described this phenomenon in her factory diary. It involves a loss of past and future, an artificially produced psychotic situation. More and more people are losing the capacity for remembering what was, and at the same time the ability to imagine a future, to have a vision. Visionless vegetating becomes the normal way of life. Hope atrophies. This form of estrangement from the self is also what we call in theological language sin: the incapacity to believe and to hope, the compulsion to remain stuck fast in sin. The disintegration and destruction of time alienates us from the area of autonomy which a person possesses if he can divide up and organize, at least potentially, and if he has wishes and dreams. Here the compulsion to sin or to live in estrangement is like a compulsion to deadness. In the modern context, sin has in general more the character of passive, unwilling letting-it-happen, not-having-done-anything-about-it, rather than a deliberate action. Our killing and stealing is in most cases unconscious and unwilling. We hardly notice that we are killing and stealing. But we are unconsciously woven into an economic context which presupposes thieves and murderers if it is to function; and it is precisely this which means the estrangement of people from themselves.

Thirdly, the working man or woman in the factory society is estranged from his or her fellows. This begins in school, where mutual help is forbidden and is punished as 'cribbing'. In West Germany, for example, school stress goes so far that a classmate who has been away ill does not have the homework that has been set passed on to him. It goes so far that friendships break up, or do not even come into being at all, under the competition of the meritocracy. Workers and white-collar employees do not know what their colleagues earn. Human relationships between different classes or income groups are as good as impossible. The class society endangers, distorts or destroys the ties between people. Everyone is alone, and that is what he ought to feel, according to widely disseminated poetry. This form of estrangement too belongs less to what we do than to what we leave undone.

In the gospel of John we are told the story of the sick people at the pool of Bethesda, who wait for an angel to come and 'trouble the water'. The person who gets into the water first is healed. Jesus talks to one of the sick who has been waiting for years. He cannot get to the water, and tells Jesus: 'Sir, I have no man to put me into the pool when the water is troubled' (John 5.7). Sin is a person's estrangement from his neighbours. The social situation is dominated by the law of sin and death as long as a sick person has to say, 'Sir, I have no man to put me into the pool.' For according to the New Testament sickness is not a private affair, which everyone has to cope with by himself. On the contrary, it is a social matter, a question for other people. But the sin that weighs us down destroys the very smallest social unit, which is not the individual, but two people. The sick man at the pool of Bethesda does at least still talk to Jesus. He says clearly why he is still sick – because he has no one at all. He calls for help. But most sick people in the First World view their bodies and what happens to them as a private matter. The machine that is worn out has to be repaired. They aren't aware of the simple connection between their sickness and their having no one. Sin is, among other things, a state in which we are blind and incapable of perception.

The fourth form of estrangement for the worker in industrial society is the estrangement from his species, from his humanity. He is estranged from what it means to be a member of the human family. In the rich First World this expresses itself as depoliticization. Since political action and activity is not demanded and expected in the working world, political capacity, human ability for concern, for just indignation, for struggle, perishes. Most people in the world of white-collar workers take no active part in what the human family is concerned about. We are cut off from the real struggles of mankind and from their real problems. What the fight against hunger means, for example, is unknown to most people.

From earliest childhood we have been used to recognize the paramountcy of manufactured products above the worker who produces them. What is important, what has to be looked after, what has to be considered, is the machine and the saleable product. This perversion is so much a matter of course that a sense of human solidarity, a feeling that we all, as the human family, have to get along with one another on one small globe, has completely died. Apartheid is not merely the work of a few reactionary racialists in South Africa. Apartheid is a way of life, the 'every man for himself' attitude. When dockers load munitions and ship bombs to countries in the Third World, they don't know what they are doing. They have no relationship to the content or substance of their work. They have no awareness of what damage they are doing, and in whose interests. They want to get finished, to take their wages and go home. As white dockers earning a good wage, their lives are cut off from the hopes and fears of mankind as a whole.

They are estranged from nature, from their own productivity, from one another, and from their humanity. This kind of estrangement certainly affects industrial workers first of all. For them, the human experience of work as a regaining of the self after its 'self-emptying' has become objectively impossible, in mass terms. Their work is meaningless or, to sum it up in a word, it is just work for a wage. The only sense of work of this kind is what one gets for it, the reward. But this simply means that the thing in itself has become meaningless. And it is not only the workers who suffer under this senselessness and estrangement. The same is true of other people who are dependent on wages too, the white-collar workers. The estrangement which was analysed at an earlier point in the industrial era has not changed, essentially speaking. It is true that physical want has been largely done away with in the wealthy countries. But it has been replaced by a psychological misery and want of a new kind. The exploitation was exported, first of all to the poorer countries, then to the growing fringe groups in the First World: minorities, people of different races, immigrant workers, the physically or mentally handicapped, and women. These groups, which represent the Third World within the First, experience estrangement directly. But even the ruling classes in a society where most of their essential relations to life are destroyed – relations to nature, to other people, to themselves – do not live without this disorder. The concept of estrangement, like the concept of sin, is not a moral edifice constructed by the intellect, in which the wicked estrange the good. It is in actual fact a total concept, which talks about the way a certain way of production has won power over the producers, and the way things that are dead have come to dominate the living. Our way of producing and organizing work makes it possible for capital to dominate us. All other interests in life and all other human needs are subordinated to the one necessity – to make more profit. Of course envy and egoism play a part, but the real problem does not lie on the individual moral level. Sin is not the characteristic weakness of individuals; it is a structuring power which dominates society. It represents a perversion of life. Dead capital dominates living men and women, who are treated like the cogs in a machine, whereas dead things are theoretically and practically honoured as if they were God, as if they were the giver of life.

We live in a world of universal marketability. The value of a thing is calculated by the amount it sells for. 'What will I get for it?' we ask, instead of 'What point does it have in itself?' The history of education in Western society is an example of this growing degradation of everything to the status of things. Education used to have a value in itself, a functional value which couldn't be bartered. For example, I went to a grammar school and read Plato when I was eighteen. For me that was enormously important, but it had no practical results. Knowledge of Plato wasn't a saleable value. Education had a value in itself. The question of how far it was marketable in addition was never directly asked. Today overt cynicism in this matter is very much greater. What I learn is seen under the standpoint of my marketability. People who have studied at particular universities and colleges and schools in Britain and the United States have different chances from the outset. Education has become part of the sales world.

At this point let me pass from a description of the situation to a theological interpretation of it. The estrangement which we experience is the sin that dominates us. According to a Christian understanding of the world, sins are not particular things we do as individuals – the infringement of sexual norms, for example. They are structures of power which rule over us, something to which we are subjected, from which we have to be liberated. It is not primarily a question of the violation of individual commandments. It is life under a different God, the God whom the New

Testament calls mammon. Sin is serving this god and participating in this destructive perversion. We are living in a civilization of injustice, as José Miranda has said. This injustice is not so much manifested in individual acts as in what we leave undone and what we allow others to do. The plundering of the Third World is a fact on which the civilization of injustice rests. By participating in this civilization we are subjected to the power of sin.

The confession that I am a sinner had little depth or power for me as long as I understood it in the framework of bourgeois individualistic theology. It was only when I realized that I am a German after Auschwitz, it was only when I began to see myself as part of the collective Germany of this century, that my theological understanding deepened. I learnt to understand myself as being a part of the collective estrangement. I participate in estrangement and introduce estrangement to others. I go along with it and pass it on. I am born into it. But I am also an active part of the civilization of injustice. According to the classical theological interpretation, sin is always both fate and guilt. In Protestantism, the character of personal guilt has always been strongly stressed. The collective fate of men and women was repressed or mythically ontologized. Instead of describing sin in its concrete historical manifestations, as the power that dominates our life, we have seen primal evil, radical evil, as an unconquerable enemy and have failed to make a more precise analysis of historical conditions. If we today introduce estrangement as a key concept, this is meant to help to overcome the interpretation of sin which was held by bourgeois Protestant theology. To understand sin as the estrangement of working people from ourselves, from their neighbour, from nature and from humanity, means that the concept that has been passed down to us has to be corrected in two different directions. We have once more to arrive at a collective understanding instead of a merely individualistic one; and our ontological interpretation has to become historical.

Sin is a power that really does make slaves of us, as Paul says (Rom. 6.20). It 'reigns' in our mortal bodies (Rom. 6.12), it has dominion over us. I can only understand all these statements and reflections of Paul's if I relate them to the collective in which I live, if I link them with the class to which I belong, with my own race and nation. The question whether I am entangled in sin actively or passively is then no longer decisive. The essential point is the question of how deep my perception of sin goes, and where I stand in the struggle against its enslaving power. Liberal Protestantism couldn't understand the total and collective dimension of sin. It certainly strengthened and deepened the individual's capacity for feeling guilt, and at the same time it confused this with an anthropological pessimism, in which the liberating traditions of faith were suppressed. Sin was then seen as a metahistorical concept. It is accordingly entirely in line with bourgeois religiosity when clergy from the pulpit and church leaders in their public utterances stress that it is impossible to change human nature, that the urge towards evil is deep and ineradicable, that man is wicked by nature and is so in every conceivable society. All these statements were, and are, used to prevent changes in society. They are used in a reactionary sense. Is this what the Bible intends when it talks about sin?

Sin is a term that describes the disturbed relationship between God and man, which leads to the disturbance of our relationship to ourselves, to our neighbours, to creation and to the human family. The Bible is not interested in saying anything about our essential nature, but defines us in the context of our relationships, describing the way they actually came to be destroyed in the era before Christ. But aren't we still living 'before Christ'? Whenever we join in the general plaint, 'You can't change human nature', we give sin power over us and deny the power of Christ over our lives. We have then made the perspectives of estrangement in which we live the only ones there are. The vulgar Protestantism which, in its secularized forms, determines the thinking of the First World, above all in its unproductive and totalized feelings of guilt, insists on the unalterability of human nature. The statement that 'With our own power we nothing can', as Luther's hymn puts it, becomes an expression of bourgeois helplessness in the face of political circumstances. This naturalistic perspective can neither think in terms of history and change, nor can it develop a profound understanding of guilt and responsibility. Let me give you an example. It is a school essay written by a twelve-year-old boy who grew up in Harlem, in New York. He was supposed to write a beast fable, with a moral at the end.

> Once a boy was standing on a huge metal flattening machine. The flattener was coming down slowly. Now this boy was a boy who loved insects and bugs. The boy could have stopped the machine from coming down but there were two lady bugs on the button, and in order to push the button he would kill the two lady bugs. The flattener was about a half inch over his head now he made a decision he would have to kill the lady bugs. He quickly pressed the button. The machine stopped, he was saved, and the lady bugs were dead.
> Moral: smash or be smashed.

This story can be read in two different ways. One way of interpreting it would be natural and ontological. Human nature is unalterable. We are unable not to sin. Life is this flattening machine and we can't do anything about it: smash or be smashed. The other way of reading this story is in what might be called a historical light. Then the story is not read for its general ontological truth. Instead we ask about the collective fate it springs from. The questions we ask here are: What is the situation of this boy out of the ghetto? What do we know about the conditions he lives in, his family relationships and his chances of work? What kind of school does he go to? And what can be said about a society in which twelve-year-old children have fantasies like this? Is this so by nature? Was it always so? Would the ancestors of this black boy in an African tribe have to invent a story like this?

There is a great deal of theological confusion about sin. Some people muddle up social Darwinism with the Christian doctrine of sin. They understand that we are living in a jungle, that we are threatened by huge omnipotent machines, like the one the little boy dreamt about. There is no way out. We are powerless. Social Darwinism is a viewpoint which sees life as a natural struggle and as 'natural selection'. Either you or me; smash or be smashed. We are dominated by a feeling of helplessness and the impossibility of changing anything in the great machine. But the estrangement we experience here is not fate; it is sin. It is not simply technological development which has led to the present situation of our world. When we feel helpless and powerless, this tells us something about ourselves, and is not merely a reflection of the given situation. It tells us something about our lack of faith.

For the opposite of sin is not moral purity. That contrast is only true of individual transgressions. I told a lie or I spoke the truth: that would be a moral contrast. But the real problem is that I am living in a world of lies, in which it is impossible to know the truth and to act accordingly. Truth's whole sphere has been taken from us, because it is impossible to search for truth or to find it if the problem of justice is ignored; the attempt is doomed to failure. This can be seen most clearly in the militarization of science[7] and its dependency on the growing militarism of society.

The feeling of powerlessness is the deepest form of estrangement which our civilization produces. We think that we are incapable of changing anything. The system in which we live presents itself as a demonic mixture of compulsion and seduction. Many people are aware of how disturbed they and their neighbours are. But the struggle seems hopeless. There is nothing that can be altered in the fundamental conditions – and, when one comes down to it, are things really so bad after all? Is all this not based on exaggeration and false expectations? I am talking about people in the First World. They often end up in a half-hearted justification of the system, a life without faith.

Faith would show a deeper trust in the reality of liberation than the one we possess. Faith would not admit the validity of social Darwinism's statement that human nature is unalterable. Faith does not mean enduring the self-estrangement; it means transcending it.

In the first three chapters of the letter to the Romans, Paul talks about sin as a power which dominates the people who have permitted that domination. People have enthroned false gods, put their own products in God's place. 'They exchanged the glory of the immortal God for images resembling mortal man or birds or animals or reptiles' (Rom 1.23). They have confused dead things with living ones; instead of loving and reverencing life they have reverenced and cultivated their own products. 'They exchanged the truth about God for a lie and worshipped and served the creature rather than the Creator' (Rom. 1.25).

To talk frankly about my own theological biography, I always had difficulty in understanding Paul here. I didn't know what the point of mythical ideas about reverencing curious birds and animals was supposed to mean nowadays – ideas deriving from a different era in the history of religion. While I was at the university I learnt that the Reformers attempted to translate what idolatry is into our own terms. They interpreted it as meaning that some people reverence sexuality or money or power instead of God, and make a god of these things. But I thought that this interpretation was rather forced and artificial, because I couldn't really see the demonic power of these idols and their absolute power, especially since the Reformers left out the Pauline collective understanding of history. The interpretation was an individualization of the interpretation of sin, and utterly un-Pauline. It was only when I encountered the Hegel-Marx tradition that I understood the truth of what Paul is talking about. Manufactured things really do have power over human beings. Production, the work of our hands, becomes the god and law-giver of our lives. The perversions of the ancient world seem relatively harmless compared with our everyday experience. Our laws protect private property. Aren't they there to protect human beings? The quality of our life in the First World is diminishing, in spite of the prosperity that still exists or is still increasing. We live under the power of the sin Paul talks about: the worship of idols on the subjective side, domination on the objective side, are the two elements in the definition of sin which Paul gives. He sums up what we ought to listen to as a message to us at the end of the twentieth century, not as if it were just an ancient document:

> None is righteous, no, not one; no one understands, no one seeks for God . . . Their feet are swift to shed blood, in their paths are ruin and misery, and the way of peace they do not know. There is no fear of God before their eyes (Rom. 3.10, 15–18).

The Christian doctrine of sin tells us that we can only recognize sin when we leave its empire, when we transcend it. The sinner himself does not understand where he is living or what is happening. He is like the rich man in a

45

German fairytale[8] who, after he has died, arrives in a beautiful place. He sleeps in a soft bed, he has wonderful things to eat, there are chests full of gold and precious stones in the cellar. But after a thousand years he becomes bored and asks: Where am I actually? Is this the heaven you praised so much? Then Peter comes down from heaven and tells him that he is in fact in hell.

As long as we are at home in the system of estrangement and sin we have no full awareness of reality.

Our education is a kind of brain-washing that keeps us from seeing. Traditional theology teaches that there is only one place in the world where we can receive our sight, and that is the cross. That is the place where I first saw the light. I was lost, I was blind, I was estranged, I worshipped the mammon who is dead instead of the living God. To talk about sin in a theological sense means talking about the past. The rich man in his palace cannot do this; he thinks he is in heaven. But who can talk about estrangement? It is the Christian, who has joined the battle, who has been liberated from his feelings of powerlessness, who has overcome his own fear. It is the Christian who comes back in order to take over what he has in common with the man from Nazareth: the cross.

3 Cross and Liberation[1]

I closed my last lecture by pointing to the cross, the place where Christians stand when they begin to be aware of the civilization of injustice, and of estrangement as sin. The cross teaches us to perceive sin. In the discipleship of the man who was tortured to death, we learn to understand our own lives.

What is the task of theology in the context of the First World? What role do Christians play in the highly industrialized rich white countries in this last quarter of the twentieth century? Where are we going? Where ought we to be going?

There is a story in the New Testament that has become more and more important for me. It is a terrible story about our class, about you and me, about our today, and perhaps about our tomorrow. A rich young man comes to Jesus and asks him: 'What must I do to inherit eternal life?' From the time he was a boy he has never stolen, robbed or murdered. Jesus likes him, and says to him: 'You lack one thing; go, sell what you have, and give to the poor . . . and come, follow me.' When the young man hears that, a cloud comes over his face and he goes away sadly (Mark 10.17–22). A terrible story about the situation of the middle classes, between the oppressors and the oppressed. A story that has been repeated. I think of the Germany of the early

30s, when many people who had been rather liberal earlier went over to the Nazis out of fear of communism, and when Hitler won the elections of 1933 with the help of what were then the Christian parties. I think too of the middle classes in Chile at the end of the Allende period, the housewives and the truck-drivers who let themselves be bribed and wanted to cling to their privileges. A terrible and depressing story. But it was told to us so that we could find our own counter-story.

What would it look like? And who helps us to find it? What meaning has a theology of liberation for the citizens of the Western world? By a theology of liberation I do not only mean the Latin American theology that goes under that name. I mean a world-wide movement of Christians, sustained by very varied groups, who are no longer prepared to use theology for the justification of existing injustice. It is an exodus theology, which makes exodus from the particular individual Egypt of oppression the real theological theme. Redemption is understood as liberation; Christ is the liberator. The building of a world in which righteousness will be possible – and therefore peace as well – is our uncompletable but also unrenounceable work for the kingdom of God. I cannot go into the ramifications of these genuine theologies here, but I will try to arrive at theological statements about the liberation of the white and wealthy middle classes of the West too, by asking the question: what does it mean to take up one's cross? I am starting from the many passages in the New Testament which talk about taking up the cross, and make that the condition of discipleship. Walter Jens[2] has translated Matthew 16. 24ff. in words which might be rendered in English as follows:

> If anyone wants to follow me,
> he must pick up the cross-beam
> on which they are going to crucify me.
> For the person who wants to keep his life
> will lose it.
> But if he loses it for my sake,
> he will keep it (Matt. 16.24ff.).

And from another passage in the same gospel (10.38):

> Anyone who loves his father and mother
> more than me
> does not belong to me.
> Anyone who does not pick up the cross-beam
> on which they are going to crucify him,
> does not belong to me.

Here is the English version of Jörg Zink's even freer translation of a passage from Mark.[3]

If anyone wants to take my way, let him not think about himself or regard his own life. Let him take the cross-beam on which they will hang him on his own shoulders and walk behind me. For the person who wants to save his life will lose it in the process; but the person who loses his life because he belongs to me and because he believes my message will find life (Mark 8.34f.).

These sayings probably date from the period when a Christian was certain of martyrdom. They are a summons to appear in court. They belong to the 'Q' period, before any of the four gospels had been compiled. These are radical demands which lead to real divisions between people, and even tear families apart. At that time people actually left their families in the name of Jesus. If the family does not expressly decide in favour of Jesus' message, Jesus' disciples must leave that family, and shake off its dust from their feet (Matt. 10.14). The call to take up the cross is a radical one. It says: Do not try to avoid the fate that is in store for you if you follow me. Luke interprets this saying by adding the word 'daily': 'Let him take up his cross daily' (Luke 9.23). This reflects a different situation, in which everyday Christian life is no longer threatened by martyrdom.

But what does this 'cross-beam on which people will hang you' mean – the gallows, the cross? It was a special mode of execution in the ancient world, a mode of execution in which the victim often died only after days of torture. It was people belonging to the lower classes who had to expect the cross – slaves, the dependent, runaways. The cross had been created for them, as an instrument to preserve power for the rulers. But it was also used as a means of disciplining the higher classes: political rebels were crucified. If we ask who could expect the cross, and which people could identify themselves with Jesus' call, to be historically correct we must answer: the lower classes who also fill our prisons today, the people who were accused of revolutionary opinions, words or acts and – on a level with them and belonging to them – the Christians.

The cross was a political instrument, an instrument of oppression. So what has political struggle to do with the cross and with faith? In order to answer that I have to widen the horizon a little. We live in a polarized, divided society. There are extreme inequalities in people's share in the total social production, inequalities compared with which the mediaeval inequality between king and beggar seems minute. Material and political privileges divide the possessors of the means of production from the dependent majority. Inequalities exist both between developed and under-developed countries, independent and dependent economic structures, and even among the wealthy peoples belonging to the industrial nations. The inequality in property, income and power is the reason behind the division into different classes. A society that is determined by class privileges necessarily produces class struggles. One cannot preserve rule that secures material privileges without fighting for it. Struggle is the natural expression of division, a fact of life in a class society.

We have thereby to distinguish between two forms of class struggle, the struggle from above and the one from below. The struggle from above is unavoidable, because it is certainly possible to live without struggle if one is subjected to bondage or slavery, but not if one is the ruler and oppressor. In order to preserve privileges, one must be alert, develop both hard and soft forms of struggle. Direct economic pressure and indirect ideological compulsion go hand in hand. An example of the first method is the refusal of many industrialists in West Germany to go on training apprentices if they cannot at the same time use them as cheap labour; an example of the second is the banning of words like 'class' or 'struggle', because they allegedly endanger the state or produce terrorism. It is impossible to preserve privileges without domination and compulsion. In this sense the cross too is a method of class struggle from above.

Class struggle from below, on the other hand, is quite simply permanent and a matter of course. The lower classes have to make a decision. By nature they tend towards political apathy and fatalism – 'Can't do anything about it; just one of those things'. Here, too, hard and soft forms of struggle have been developed, but we should not forget that the most important weapon of the working class has been a non-violent one – the strike: the unarmed worker against heavily armed police and military units at the service of the privileged classes. We must learn to see the struggle as a fact in the face of which no neutrality is possible. The only question that counts is on which side you stand.

Yet the avoiding tactic of the class to which I too belong – the middle class – is neutralization. Objectivity and non-partisanship are educational goals which we have internalized. But a clear awareness of the role, the task and the importance of the middle classes is lacking. Middle-class people prefer not to decide. They see themselves as standing above the conflict. They waver in their sympathies and adherences. A young minister or teacher in a poor area will have very mixed feelings. On the one hand they will recognize the needs of the population and want to identify themselves with their cause. The teacher also wants a smaller class and better equipment. On the other hand she has been trained to expect everything from the powerful bureaucracy above her. Is she responsible to the children or to the authorities? In most cases she will try to avoid making a decision, or will only act half-heartedly. For that is what she has learnt to do. The crudely fundamental question 'Which side are you on?' is not a favourite one. The wavering of the middle classes certainly has its good side as well: its openmindedness, its capacity for learning, its openness towards both sides. But the danger of the middle-class situation is eternal indecision.

Kierkegaard criticized this type of person under the heading of 'endless reflection', which makes a person incapable of arriving at a decision and facing up to reality. The intellectual and religious neutrality which fears to make a decision for or against faith and continually puts the decision off is not very far removed from the intellectual and political neutrality by means of which an intellectual tries to keep out of conflicts – in his university, perhaps, or the newspaper he writes for. Religious and political neutrality are two aspects of the same attitude. Reflection, hesitation in forming a judgment, and scepticism are frequently encouraged by a better-than-average education. Kierkegaard criticized this attitude in scathing terms: the freedom and non-commitment which is allegedly cherished in this way turns into bondage. Neutrality is impossible. The person who doesn't make up his mind has made it up already.

Perhaps you are irritated by the way I continually mix up politics and religion. Am I talking about Kierkegaard or about class struggle? It is becoming increasingly difficult for me and for many other Christians to separate the two. I can no longer pigeon-hole my life in this way. I know with certainty that the gospel can endure no neutrality, no opting out. One may hesitate to give the name of class struggle to Jesus' struggle against his people's own ruling class, the Sadducees, and against Rome's imperialist oppression; but there is no doubt at all on which side he stood: on the side of the poor, the people who were religiously uneducated and therefore despised – women, for instance – the outcasts, like the whores and the tax-collectors. He recruited his friends from fishermen, who were the rural proletariat. The aim of his struggle – the kingdom of God – meant overcoming a class society and turning it into one where brotherhood and sisterhood are possible. The call to take up the cross is the call to join the struggle. Take sides, break with your neutrality, put yourself on the side of the damned of this world.

This interpretation of the call 'take up your cross and follow me' of course contradicts a bourgeois interpretation. When the martyr's cross of the primitive church ceased to have any meaning, the cross was spiritualized and made an affair of everyday life. We can already see this in Luke. Taking up one's cross was interpreted as denying oneself, as not giving in to one's own wishes. The fact that the cross was an instrument of torture in the class struggle from above seemed forgotten. In bourgeois theology the cross is narrowed down to personal life, and what happens to one there. A life-long illness, perhaps, or an unhappy

53

marriage, or a profession one dislikes – these are the things that are looked on as the crosses that people have to take on themselves. What can't be cured must be endured, bear it with patience, accept what is laid on you. I cannot find much biblical foundation for this prevailing exegesis, especially when it doesn't speak to men and women in the midst of their active life but appeals to them solely in 'limit' situations. Moreover is falsifies the act of decision involved in laying hold of the wood of the cross and taking it, converting this into a mere responsive act of acceptance of what is already lying on the shoulders of the person who is summoned in this way. Did Jesus then exhort us to endurance, instead of sending us into battle? Is 'submit to your fate' the same thing as 'Take up your cross and follow me'?

If we leave bourgeois theology behind us, we must give up the individualistic framework within which it works. Individualism, as the deepest and ultimate category, is the premise of bourgeois theology. 'When all is said and done', I often hear educated Protestants say (whether they are 'still' in the church or whether they are not in the church 'any more') – 'when all is said and done, everyone is alone with his God.' Here the cross is seen as the cry of loneliness, as suffering over life, over guilt, over finitude and death. But this robs the cross of its political dimension.

A new interpretation, which thinks of the cross and political struggle together, begins with the active, conscious decision of a life for the poor and oppressed. With the cross Jesus did not either simply take upon himself a fate which he had to accept and endure. He left his Father's house of his own free will. It was his own decision to leave Galilee, where he undoubtedly had stronger support. In the end he went freely towards his own catastrophe, which we call the cross, no differently from thousands of organized workers, who could also lead a more peaceful and tranquil life at home.

I should like to develop three dimensions of what it means to take up one's cross. It means:

breaking with neutrality;
making the invisible visible;
sharing a vision.

It is decision, compassion and vision. The first step is to break with the neutrality we have been trained to. To use the language of the exodus symbol: neutrality comes from Egypt. It is Pharaoh who teaches us to think neutrally and not one-sidedly, respecting the technological realities. Of course Pharaoh is not completely wrong but his viewpoint springs from the existing culture of injustice and his goal is to ameliorate this injustice without altering the system. Christ's viewpoint, on the other hand, is extremist and one-sided because his view in any given situation is always that of the victim. Christ sees the world with the eyes of the victimized, and it is this very one-sidedness which took him to the cross. 'Take up your cross and follow me' means: join the battle. Give up your neutrality. Leave the standpoint that wavers between the old and the new world. What, then, did Jesus really fight for? Why couldn't he stay peacefully at home in Nazareth? Why didn't he simply fulfil the expectations the people of his time had about his role: obedience to the law, reverence for the dead, loyalty to the family, and the worship of a God who will look after everything else? Why wasn't that enough for him?

Jesus must have felt that the expectation he encountered about the role he had to play, and this form of life, were a kind of death, a being cut off from transcendence. He organized resistance against this death, the middle-class death of an orderly life in a nice house. His God was far from being the one who is responsible for a few remaining, fringe problems in a world that is in principle well ordered. His God stood up for the lives of the people to whom life, a full stomach, work, being able to develop one's talents, and learning were all denied. 'He has filled the hungry with good things, and the rich he has sent empty away' (Luke 1.53). Jesus did not live his life in the simple expectation that the miracle which the Magnificat talks about would be brought to pass some day or other, through some supernatural power. That would be mythology in the bad sense of the word, and would make life something fixed and objective, a thing. Jesus saw himself as part of the energy which consummates the profoundest intentions of history towards liberation, and he acted accordingly. His struggle was to let these hopes become realities in his own time.

Christ didn't preach submission and resignation to the exploited. He didn't bring the peace of the three wise monkeys, who close their eyes, their ears and their mouths, in order not to have heard anything and not to have seen anything; so that they don't have to say anything, and don't have to echo the cries of the oppressed and the tortured. Christ didn't come to bring peace but a sword (Matt. 10.30), as we are told in the context of the call to take up the cross. He didn't bring the Kissinger peace, in which ruling injustice is guaranteed by police force. No peace is possible between people who are hungry and others who have over-eaten themselves. The absence of war, which is what we are accustomed to call peace, requires violent and brutal forms of oppression. This talk of the sword, of the neutrality of silence that has to be broken, the call of Christ to take up the cross, is not abstract. You will know what I mean. I am thinking of all the people who have broken with neutrality and have stopped believing that middle-class values – neutrality, a non-party attitude, detachment, individualism – are the supreme ones. I am thinking of the people who have stopped enduring the violation of the human dignity of the person who stands beside them. I am thinking of the people whose fate we do not know. Let us never forget that they are in Christ, because they have taken hold of his cross and are carrying it. 'He who loses his life will find it.'

The humane character of this struggle springs from an all-embracing compassion. To see the victims in any given situation means making the invisible visible. In our society – and I am again talking about West Germany – people are becoming invisible, persons are becoming non-persons, with the help of economic, social and political structures which are simultaneously exploitive and disguising. People who have shares in South African concerns generally don't know that their money is helping to keep up both profits and infant mortality. People who eat Outspan oranges or who buy diamonds don't know that these things are blood-stained, tainted with the blood of the murdered school children in Soweto. It is part of the civilization of injustice to make its victims invisible.

At the time of Jesus the people who were invisible in this sense were the people who didn't know the law and were poor, with all that that involved – imprisonment for debt, the selling of the family, forced labour. Jesus fought against an order which counted the life and health of these people as of less value than the preservation of the kind of order found in the laws about the observance of the sabbath, for instance. He attached only relative value to natural ties; he criticized family and filial love. What is a father's funeral compared with the struggle for the kingdom of God? A new brotherliness replaced the old family relationships, which are so often used to let the invisible people, who are outside the clan, go on being invisible. 'Who are my mother and my brothers?' asked Jesus, and he included in his family the people who participated in his struggle and his provocation (Mark 3.35). His friends belonged to the ignorant, illiterate masses.

I am not using the word struggle for Jesus and what he did in order to appeal to armed force. There are a great many different forms of struggle, and the individual terror of a few extremists such as we experienced in West Germany a few years ago has nothing whatsoever to do, in goal or methods, with the struggle that brought Jesus to the cross. I am using the word in order to make clear Jesus' militancy, as his opponents felt it to be. And in order to understand Jesus, we must first of all put ourselves on the side of his potential opponents. As a German, I belong to one of the richest and best-armed nations in a world full of starving people. To make visible the people who are invisible and who have been hushed up belongs to the continuing process of revelation. 'No man has ever seen God; if we love one another, God abides in us and his love is perfected in us' (I John 4.12). In this way what before was invisible becomes visible.

This brings me to the third dimension of the cross; the shared vision. It is not enough to have an individual dream of a better life. We need a communicated dream. We need the remembrance of victories that have already been won. It is only in this way (contrary to the total forgetfulness of history which accompanies late capitalism) that we live from our roots in history. The victims of earlier times are with us and their unheard cries are still waiting for an answer. No one is forgotten and no tears have been shed in vain. The Christian interpretation of history knows a goal, a vision which is certainly not simply identical with the socialist vision of a classless society, but which cannot under any circumstances mean anything less than a society without domination. Without this shared vision it would be impossible to take up the cross. It is this vision which is our strength. Here I am speaking for all those who at this very moment are being tortured or are in prison, waiting for the next interrogation. I am speaking for the growing number of priests and nuns, Christians and people who have long since ceased to find a home in the churches, who have followed the call of Jesus, have taken up the cross on which others will crucify them. If there is hope anywhere for the churches, then it is embodied in these men and women. I am talking like this because I think it is important that we should think of them now, because I believe that our remembrance of them – which we can also call prayer – helps them and supports them even into the darkness about which we can only be silent.

But this knowledge and this remembrance helps us too in our perhaps less dramatic struggles. The little group, the grass roots community, the cell, which goes a little way along the road with Jesus, needs the assurance that it is not alone. Jesus says 'I and the Father are one' (John 10.30). We should stop hearing these words in an exclusively christological sense. They are talking about the profound strength which is given to us in the struggle, the experience of wholeness and of being reunited with mankind and their real hopes. We were cut off, we were living behind the wall of apartheid which is built out of prosperity and blindness; but now we can see. We were separated from our brothers and sisters who hunger and thirst after righteousness and justice, but now we are united, because we are fighting for them and at their side. We were individualized, sunk in the aesthetic refinement of bourgeois music and poetry, but now we are free to share with others the strength that comes from beauty. What can't be shared isn't worth possessing. In this way the riches of our culture will come alive for the present in a new sense. In this way we transcend the frontiers of our individual strength, which is so quickly used up, and the limits of our own brief lives. We need more hope than we have to hand and, God knows, more love than what we take and give at present. No other transcendence has been promised to us except the transcendence that comes about in the cross.

I should like to close with a verse from the American hymnbook, a witness to the piety of earlier generations, which in very simple words describes a basic Christian experience. However individualistically it may have been meant, we as Christians have the liberty and the right to stand up as co-authors of the tradition and to make the old words our own.

> At the cross, at the cross,
> Where I first saw the light,
> And the burden of my heart rolled away –
> It was there by faith
> I received my sight,
> And now I am happy all the day.[4]

It is at the cross that we first see the light, not when we are born or when we see the sea or the stars for the first time. It is at the cross, in the midst of the battle, where we experience the light and are freed from our fears. The burden of sin, our powerlessness in estrangement, rolls away from our hearts. At the cross, where love fights against violence, we receive our life's perspectives. We learn to accept ourselves as fighting and as suffering. The light is with us.

4 Christ – The Dignity of Men and Women

The subject of this lecture is the insulted dignity of men and women and its restoration in Christ. Let me briefly outline the way we have come, up to now.

For us, faith means resisting cynicism in a situation that is objectively cynical. Faith has a militant power, which grows in the struggle against objective cynicism. As long as we put up with estrangement, we reproduce it and pass it on to other people. In this sense participating in estrangement means living under sin. What we need is a perception of the sin which is the destruction of our relationship to nature, to our neighbour and to ourselves. The perception of sin is contrition and conversion. But we only arrive at conversion when we expose ourselves to suffering and struggle. That is why the cross and participation in the struggle for righteousness and justice is the place where Christians receive their sight. In this way the prayer 'Strengthen our faith' is another way of saying 'Do not let us sink into cynicism'. In this way the prayer for recognition of our own situation is a prayer for awareness about our own lives. When Christians meditate together on the cross, they are not interested in a contemplative enjoyment of all that Christ has done for us. Their purpose is participation, identification. Let us choose the cross, the struggle. The imperative for today is: see what Christ gives – the dignity of men and women. I should again like to start from the situation in the First World and try to say something about the particular destruction of human dignity in a consumer society.

When he was talking about the inexorable repression which the soft violence of consumer culture imposes on people, Pasolini wrote: 'There is in fact no longer anything religious in the ideal picture of the young man and woman propagated and ordained by television. They are simply two people whose lives now only find expression by way of consumer goods.'[1]

What does the statement 'no longer anything religious' mean? Was the ideal picture of a young couple surrounded by a different aura in earlier times? Did it have a different content? Was any happiness promised beyond the happiness of consuming together? The loss of expressiveness means being cut off from any kind of transcendence. According to the scheme of things so forcefully presented by television, the young couple whose life finds its expression in consuming, no longer even feel the need for a language to formulate their own pain and their own desires. Life itself is not in any way at stake; in fact its value is simply dependent on how much one can buy and how long one can go on buying at all. 'Those empty shop windows, that lack of colour – life isn't worth living over there', one hears American tourists say when they have been visiting eastern European countries. Pasolini calls consumerism the new fascism because it destroys all humanist values, softly, without the application of physical force, simply by means of its new techniques of information and communication. When the age of bread is past, what point is there in sharing bread and wine with one another? 'It is obvious that superfluous goods make life superfluous.'[2]

The young man and woman on television, who no longer have anything religious about them, are without grace, without mercy. They need no mercy, they expect none. It doesn't occur to anyone to say, 'God have mercy on them' when he looks at them. It was this promise, this hope, this wish, which expressed itself in our culture by means of this young couple. An aura of fragile happiness used to surround these young people, and made them 'touching', as the phrase still went. We cannot even wish today's ideal TV couple '*Masel tov!*' or 'Best of luck!' Why should we? After all, they can buy whatever they want. So the wish freezes on our lips and the icy cold of all the relationships that have been freed of longing and desire radiates from the TV screen into every living room.

In the consumer culture, happiness is defined as having, not being. This 'having' goes through different phases and styles, from the quiet bon vivant to the energetically active hero. In Europe, where the transition to consumerism is going on, one can see how the older values of middle-class culture are being abolished: thrift, family life, altruism are all being systematically undermined by advertising. 'You've a right to give yourself a treat', we are told. Today advertisement is no longer addressed to the anal accumulator so much as to the genital conqueror. He is becoming the chief model. Happiness is not accumulating and devouring; it is possessing, occupying something that used to be occupied and possessed by other people. It is no longer the goods but the selling of them which is at the centre of advertising. Possession is becoming a lust. And consequently the main element which religious tradition drew upon in trying to describe happiness – the experience of grace – is becoming incomprehensible to an increasing degree.

Grace is a concept which describes the depths of our

possible happiness. When I choose life in existential absol-uteness, when integration and decision coincide, when I have given my assent to the great 'yes' and have become practised in the struggle against cynicism, then I have an experience which underlies all true happiness, in so far as happiness has become capable of utterance in the culture that has come down to us. I notice that it is not what I have achieved that has brought me into this condition – the condition which actually liberates the goals of my own wishes. I do not dispose over my 'yes'. I am not the boss and I forget that I ever wanted to be so. 'Non-disposability' is a category of existential philosophy which forgets itself at its peril. Every real 'yes' is responsive, and this respon-sive character belongs to the experience of happiness in general. Happiness means cor*respond*ing to someone or to a situation, not merely speaking. It is integration in the play of give and take. It is not just taking, getting, pos-sessing, or pure acting, doing or giving. It is grace, and the more grace is experienced in any happiness, the deeper it is.

How can I know this? someone may ask – perhaps a younger listener, less affected by the religious tradition. The limitations of my language, I would reply, are the limitations of my world. The wealth of my language is the wealth which I can experience. The tradition in which I stand has given me a language with interprets my own experience, clarifies it, makes it transparent and enriches it. One of its words, grace, contains a conception of hap-piness which seemed to be more enticing than what was offered to me otherwise. I found my capacity for wishing respected, my fears dealt with, my need for significance taken infinitely seriously. My capacity for happiness grew with my capacity for speech (and my capacity for pain too, but that belongs in my tradition under the heading of 'contrition'.) That is why I find consumerism an attack on my human dignity and think that genocide – the word which Pasolini uses for it – is no exaggeration.

Consumerism represents an attack on human dignity unprecedented in human history, which has been economically determined by want and the struggle to survive. I don't want you to get the impression that these questions are the luxury problems of people who have nothing else to worry about. Human dignity can be insulted in different ways. When we say that it is Christ who stands as a poor woman with her children on the fringe of the slums, raking through the rubbish, we can also say that it is Christ who screams in psychosis and tears his face with his nails before they put him in a straitjacket and quieten him down with injections. Human dignity is indivisible. That fact was perhaps never as clear as it is today, in a global culture of dependency. There is a profound connection between the injustice which the citizens of the industrial world commit by means of restrictive tariffs, the international division of labour and the manipulation of the world market, and the West's own psychological misery. The material misery of the Third World and the psychological misery of the West belong together, economically, politically and ecologically – and culturally and psychologically as well. To establish this connection and to make it evident is a theological task for our time. We are all suffering from the same cancer. Human dignity is being insulted in both places, even if in different ways. And in both parts of the world we can see how Christ restores the insulted dignity of men and women and makes them again capable of action and suffering, where they were previously only the passive victims of what was done to them.

The consumer culture brings with it an almost complete destruction of the language in which people were able to communicate with one another. For real communication can only come into being where people can express their needs and wants. But it is at this very point that the most profound disturbance of language is taking place, because our needs are being manipulated. In the barter society everything has its price, as we know. And every need has its material substratum. There is no longer any language for communicating in a convincing way about meaning, faith and struggle, because all our essential or existential needs are hushed up or manipulatively exchanged for something else. In our culture 'being' is replaced by 'having'. In a newspaper I read an advertisement for a heating system, which began with the words: 'Warmth for a lifetime!' The potential buyers the advertisement appealed to were poor and elderly people whose elemental need really is for warmth. But they are cheated of the fulfilment of this need by having something else foisted on to them instead; and this is the way all advertising goes about things. Our need *to be*, to be with one another, to communicate, to experience solidarity and human warmth, are first titillated and then turned into needs which can be satisfied by having and buying. Our wish for a different kind of being, for becoming new, for an assurance of significance, is manipulated into a wish to change the objects of our consumerism, to possess something different, to verify and judge ourselves by what we have. Today this manipulation of the mind, this being trained to destroy one's own wishes, no longer comes about through powerful hierarchies in church and religion, but by means of production and advertising. Consumerism is the new religion.

A seventeen-year-old boy told me how, after several attempts, he got his father to agree to have a talk with him. When his father finally found a little time for his son, he opened the conversation by saying, 'Well, how much is it to be?' The father found anything else inconceivable. His son left the room and soon afterwards the house.

The dignity of men and women is always infringed wherever essential human needs are denied. The dimension of significance belongs as uniquely to human life as the dimension of space does to stars and stones. The need for significance is no less elemental than the material needs for food and shelter which we have in common with other living things. The language in which I can best talk about the meaning of my life is the language of faith, the Christian language. It helps me to articulate my hopes. The experiences which men and women have had with this language, the experiences which have been transmitted in it, encourage me and help me to overcome my lack of faith, my frustration, my subjective cynicism. I find the dignity of my humanity articulated in Christ.

What does this 'in Christ' mean? Why am I a Christian?[3] For to say I am a Christian is not simply a description of a reality, in the way that it is a reality that I am white or German or a mother. Here, to say 'I am' is as much as to say 'I am trying, I am living in that direction, I am becoming'. 'Lord, I want to be a Christian in my heart', as one of the spirituals says. I am calling myself after a person who was tortured to death 2,000 years ago, a person whom it proved impossible to kill. I am identifying myself with him. I trust his truth more than other fragments of truth which I have come to see, and certainly more than my own. I 'identify' myself, which means: I cannot describe my identity without talking about him. To be 'I' merely as white, German, a mother, a teacher, a writer, or whatever else – that would be too little for me, because it says nothing about this identification, this specific interpretation of what it means to become a person. If I avoid talking about being a Christian, then I am in danger of only saying what is, and it is just that that is too little. More belongs to my identity than my individual existence. Indeed this 'is' description is a prison which we have to leave. Transcendence is a necessary daily act. I don't stop where my arms end, just as I don't begin simply where I was born. We are only alive when we transcend. That means that we can learn to perceive the daily act of transcending, that we begin to notice the movements in which human life creates itself, the moments in which a person's face becomes the face of a person. This also means that we begin to notice the material and spiritual conditions in which their living character is taken away from people, the conditions in which they are cut off from transcendence: through hunger and misery, which directs all a person's energies towards survival, so that nothing is left for living; through the situation created by estranged work in a senseless waste of energy; through existence in consumerism, in which our life and being expresses itself merely as getting and having. The dignity of human beings is the capacity for going beyond what exists.

Christ invites us to participate in this mystery. He re-creates this very potentiality in us once more. We are people, he says, not machines, not mere producers of the gross national product, not agents of a 'national security' which has been turned into the golden calf, not merely creatures subjected to the forces of the system. On the contrary, we are capable of transcendence, because our lives are bound up with the lives of others. There is a unity between life – the human life which each of us possesses – and transcendence. That is a basic statement of Christian anthropology. I am bound-up-with, I belong-to, therefore I am. All other possible grounds for my existence, such as the Cartesian one (I think, therefore I am) or the one Albert Camus gives (I rebel, therefore I am) begin for me at too late a point. It is only because I am bound up with everyone in Christ that thinking has any purpose, and it is for this reason that I am compelled to offer resistance.

I am a Christian because of Christ. Let me try to develop

this statement, in its premises and its content. It contains a presupposition of a philosophical kind which affects the interpretation of reality. To be real means to be related, to live in relationship, to live by and in the direction of relationships. The more relationship the more reality, the less relationship the more death. This relationality means that we always already live with, by, and in the shadow of 'images' – earlier images of life, or images transmitted by other people. I cannot conceive how one can become a person without images, models, forms and voices, which speak to me. To have images, to bear images within one's mind, to be drawn by images is a part of the process we call education. Indeed the much misused but indispensable German word for education is *Bildung*, which comes from *Bild*, the picture or image. It is by living in relationships and by absorbing images, which form and change me, that I become educated. Many people, frightened of ideologies, dream of an existence free of images; but this seems to me impossible. The illusion of being able to live without images is dangerous, because it overlooks the real power which images have. Here the old theological perception applies: that the place where God is not is not simply nothingness, but a place where idols are rampant. The fetishism of science, which is the illusion of being able to live without images, prepares the space for idols. In this sense there is no life free of religion, because there is no life free of images, no life without projection. We are always already in relationships which mould us and challenge us. We always already live with, and in the shadow of, images which console us and promise significance. The question that counts is only what challenges, what consolation and what promises the images can offer us.

In an abbreviated culture it is not easy to express the necessity and productivity of images. A passage in Salinger's *Franny and Zooey* occurs to me, in which an image in the sense in which I am using the word here emerges. The image is called 'the Fat Lady'. Seymour explains to his younger brother and sister, who are to take part in the radio programme 'Wise Child', that they are to be funny for the Fat Lady, or shine their shoes for her:

'He never did tell me who the Fat Lady was, but I shined my shoes for the Fat Lady every time I went on the air again – all the years you and I were on the program together, if you remember. I don't think I missed more than just a couple of times. This terribly clear, clear picture of the Fat Lady formed in my mind. I had her sitting on this porch all day, swatting flies, with her radio going full-blast from morning till night. I figured the heat was terrible, and she probably had cancer and – I don't know. Anyway it seemed goddam clear why Seymour wanted me to shine my shoes when I went on the air. It made *sense*.'[4]

The picture which Franny forms of the Fat Lady is very like her brother's:

'I didn't ever picture her on a porch, but with very – you know – very thick legs, very veiny. I had her in an *aw*ful wicker chair. She had cancer too, though, and she had the radio going full-blast all day! Mine did, too!'

This image of the Fat Lady is now contrasted with the world of television, or

'a goddam Broadway theatre, complete with the most fashionable, most well-fed, most sunburned-looking audience you can imagine. But I'll tell you a terrible secret – Are you listening to me? *There isn't anyone out there who isn't Seymour's Fat Lady.* That includes your Professor Tupper, buddy. And all his goddam cousins by the dozens. There isn't anyone *any*where that isn't Seymour's

Fat Lady. Don't you know that? Don't you know that goddam secret yet? And don't you know – *listen* to me, now – *don't you know who that Fat Lady really is?* . . . Ah, buddy, Ah buddy. It's Christ himself. Christ himself, buddy.'

For joy, apparently, it was all Franny could do to hold the phone, even with both hands.

For a fullish half minute or so, there were no other words, no further speech. Then: 'I can't talk any more, buddy.' The sound of a phone being replaced in its catch followed.

The present day's hostile attitude to religion is connected with its fear of images, of images that can change lives. We don't want the Fat Lady because she's a nuisance, and we have to look for a great novelist like Salinger to make the connection between the Fat Lady, Christ, and all of us clear.

But in the light of this image we can perhaps say more clearly how we can distinguish images from one another, and what criteria we have for evaluating them. For it would be stupid to admit only the images of a particular era in the history of religion – the Mariolatry of the late middle ages, for example – or to confine ourselves to a necessarily limited religious world.

The criterion we can draw on to help us to distinguish God from idols cannot be defined formally. It is simply a question of content. Slogans like 'Jesus alone', 'Only Jesus', 'One way' are formalistic, because they make their Jesus a heavenly figure hovering above us without any specific content. Moreover they are exclusive, in that they reject other images. They deny that the Fat Lady is Christ. But in this way they encourage the tendency present in Christianity (as in every other religion that has become historically relevant) to turn Christ into an idol, whom one serves by crying 'Lord, Lord' to him (Matt. 7.21), but without saying specifically what is supposed to be so powerful and overwhelming about Jesus. The criterion which the Bible offers for distinguishing true from false images, and God from idols, is a matter of content. God is love, as the First Epistle of John tells us. And the image of Jesus shows us what that means. The images that are idols are the ones which have no share in this love and consequently no share in this suffering either. One can easily imagine images other than, of all things, the blood-smeared face of the one for whose sake many people call themselves 'Christian': lovelier, wiser, happier figures and pictures. The photo of a beautiful young women beside the swimming pool of a 'luxury residence' would be an idol of this kind, if it had a 'formative' function and educated people to this kind of aim in life and this kind of consolation – an idol seducing us to idolatry that is specifically capitalist.

It seems to me to be neither chance nor a trick of communist propaganda that the photo of Che Guevara which has gone round the world and which possesses a kind of ikon quality looks so much like Christ. This is due to a profound harmony of cause. It is not Che who is an idol, but all the images which deny and exclude suffering, struggle, and hence love. Our civilization tends to exclude particular images – for example, those depicting age, pain and death. We prefer images of smartness, success and 'one-upmanship'.

The choice of images that are offered is no longer dictated by tradition, and in this sense there is no possible doubt that the Christianity which was unreflectively taken over from tradition has no longer any future in the industrial civilizations. We can choose between different images as a way of formulating our lives; and we have to choose.

The fact that I am a Christian means in this modern context that I have made, and am making again, a particular choice for an image that has been passed down to us. I am going to try to live with this image. I will accept this voice. I will analyse and come to terms with this tradition for myself, accept it or reject it. This conscious decision is a mark of modern Christianity. It only becomes necessary when one has left the village in which family, custom and religion represented a self-evident structure of rule which was transferred to the inner life as well.

Why do I need this decision? The hymn I have quoted from the culture of Black American piety says in its second verse: 'Lord, I want to be more loving in my heart.' I am a Christian because I share this wish with all other Christians. I want to learn to be more loving; I want to be different from what I am; I want to diminish the distance between me and Christ; I want to live and realize righteousness, justice and love, the basic values of the Jewish and Christian tradition; I want to share in that tradition; I want to help to build up the kingdom of God, in which righteousness, justice and love exist for everyone and are open to everyone. This process, in which I become more capable of love, constitutes my life; this movement towards the kingdom of God is life's meaning. 'Christ' now stands for this movement; for its pain, for its defeats, for its miracles, for its spirit. For death. For the resurrection. Christ stands for Jesus of Nazareth plus all those who belong to him. One can then call this Christ anonymous or cosmic; it seems to me more important not to lose sight of his historical side, for this is the corrective to mystic union. The voice of the man they tortured to death couldn't be silenced. I am a Christian by yielding myself to this dialogue and this process.

'Lord, I want to be more loving.' When I sing this hymn, when I make this prayer my own, then the question 'Why Jesus? Why not Socrates or Buddha?' becomes less and less important. This question comes from the time when men and women left their religious village and discovered with astonishment that other people were living where the village left off. For those of us who grew up in the cities, religiously speaking, this is somewhat of a rearguard action, an engagement no longer in the forefront of the battle. For us, the real question is not: Why Christ, and not another image, another voice which talks to me about love and righteousness? The real question is: Why still Christ up there, out there, above us, and why not I, here and now? I do not deny that Christ is initially often a form of the super-ego who – because of the appalling superficiality of Christianization – remains nothing but a super-ego idol which generally dies later on. But in spite of this, the trend of real Christianization may be described as incarnation. Christ desires to become flesh, in me as well. Where the super-ego existed, where the mechanism of domination and control functioned, there I am to be; there the dialogue is to take place between 'I' and the I-ideal which I am talking about here, the dialogue whose deepest import is to become more like Christ.

When I ask the question: 'Why particularly this Christ and not other possible figures?' I am still imprisoned in the religious supermarket. There is nothing against this enriching supermarket of present possibilities, which widens our horizon. But can I reduce myself to the role of onlooker, admirer (as Kierkegaard put it), the religious customer? The decisive thing is not the number of images we have, but the relationship in which we stand to these images, the power we give them over our life and our world. As long as we withdraw from this question into abstractions, we are still in the supermarket without relationships, where all religions are the suppliers of consumer objects.

I am a Christian because of Christ. And to get involved with Christ means becoming like him, becoming more like him. That is why the next verse of the hymn which I am following here runs: 'Lord, I want to be like Jesus in my heart.' To identify oneself isn't a formal act, like the act of baptism, for example. It is a living process in which the lover comes to resemble the beloved more and more closely. I am a Christian so as to become like Christ. This is the way I learn best to seek the kingdom of God and to see everything else which does not serve justice and righteousness as secondary.

> Lord, I want to be a Christian in my heart.
> Lord, I want to be more loving in my heart.
> Lord, I want to be more holy in my heart.
> Lord, I want to be like Jesus in my heart.

I am a Christian for the sake of the kingdom of God. I could certainly use other names here for the kingdom of God, and I could employ other formulas which are essentially based on negative statements – the formula about the classless society, for example. To talk about the kingdom of God certainly means talking about the end of private property, injustice and domination; but we do not yet arrive at the way in which Jesus talked in his parables about the strength of the weak, and the importance of the powerless, by using critical and negative language. Negative theology reiterates and emphasizes: Not like this; this wasn't what was meant. But is the essential thing about the kingdom of God utterable at all in the medium of criticism?

I suspect we need talk about the kingdom of God as we need the image of the tormented Christ. There is no reasonable justification for giving up these words and images, gestures and ritual – in short, the tradition – provided that we are at one in our wish to be more loving and in our need for the kingdom of God. If we start from these wishes and needs, then there is a new interest in the peace that is above all understanding, a new need for a language that promises more than what is essentially critical. The language of this peace that is above critical reason is then a narrative and parable-like language. The kingdom of God is like a sower going forth to sow. We need a reminder of liberation, and stories of liberation.

Stories of this kind also help us against what is still the most obvious misunderstanding of Christianity – the interpretation which views it as if it were Platonism for the people, to use Nietzsche's phrase. As if the kingdom of God were a second world above this one, and another time after this time, and a special history of salvation which runs unscathed through the world's history of disaster. I am not speaking here for Christians who have inherited their Christianity; I am speaking for the people who have passed from naivety through the phase of criticism to a third stage of critical, selective affirmation. And in the reality of a faith like this the understanding of a controlling and all-powerful God and the hope for a life after death only play the part which they play in some of the central stories of the New Testament – which is to say none at all. I am thinking of the story of the Good Samaritan (Luke 10.25–37), of the story of the Last Judgment (Matt. 25). The assumption of a heavenly being and the hope for continuation never become the theme of these stories; whereas the subjects we have been talking about certainly do: the wish to be more and more completely loving, the interest in the kingdom in which the hungry will be filled with good things and the rich will be sent empty away (Luke 1.53). The Samaritan tries to be more completely present for another person. He doesn't stare at Jesus as if he were a mighty superstar who will put everything right. Even less does he look towards God Almighty. But he is going to act like this Jesus. In this sense he is a Christian, who needs no formal confession of faith in Christ. The old question whether the kingdom of God cannot be sought and built even without Jesus –

the question why we should be tied to Christian language – is not decided here either formally or argumentatively. The power of images and their potential for communication can only be proved in practice. One doesn't arrive at faith through books and deductions from ideas. Faith comes through common practice. Christian existence is communicated by other Christians.

There is a sentence in the Bible which has become very important in the labour movement particularly. It runs: 'All things are possible to him who believes (Mark 9.23). When the Lip clock factory at Besançon was taken over by the workers, a young man climbed up the front of the building and wrote these old words on the factory: '*Tout est possible.*' Whether the young man knew the ancient book from which this statement comes is unimportant. The important thing is that we learn it, and that this kind of language, which doesn't merely promise hope but actually creates it, does not perish.

I am a Christian if I believe that everything is possible. The blind learn how to see, old Nazis stop suppressing their past, technocrats listen to the powerless. The lame walk, the deaf hear, the poor hear the news of liberation. Perhaps at this point one must leave the individualist tone of the spiritual and go over from the 'I' to the 'we', from voluntarism into the experiences of history. I am a Christian because I believe that what was promised to everyone is possible.

Jesus of Nazareth tried to do with his life something that I want to do too, something which is for me really all important. Since the result of his experiment is uncertain, the essential thing is that as many people as possible – if possible, everyone – should work for it: by working miracles, by suffering, by telling, by sharing.

He is my brother who, since he is a little older than me, is always a death ahead of me; who, since he is a little younger than me, and madder than me, is always a miracle ahead of me.

What does he do for me? I learn from him. When one has ceased to learn one is dead, and it is from him that I learn most. He talks about my life in the way I want him to talk, without any contempt. He doesn't allow a single day of my life to be held cheap, doesn't allow it to be meaningless or without the great experiment. I learn from him to overcome all cynicism. I find this the most difficult lesson today. For there are convincing reasons for despising people. There are excellent reasons for despising myself. There is a temptation to affirm life only partially, for only a little way, only under certain circumstances. He puts me to shame – my limited, impatient, partly superficial affirmation. He teaches me an infinite, a revolutionary 'yes' which doesn't leave out anything or anybody at all.

5 Resurrection and Liberation

The purpose of the Christian religion is that, believing, we 'may have life in his name' (John 20.31). This sentence is to be found at the end of the account of Christ's resurrection in the gospel of John. It is life in this world that is being talked about here, a real, authentic life, in which we become more and more free of fear and more and more capable of love. 'Life' doesn't mean just vegetating, just about surviving, the permanent suffocation which we often experience life as being. Life is as if a mother smiles at her daughter and asks 'Are you happy?' Or as if a schoolboy, riding his bicycle home, takes his hands off the handlebars and throws his arms in the air. When we talk about the resurrection of the dead we mean this possible, fulfilled life. I John 5.13 might be translated: 'I write this to you that you may know that you have eternal life because you believe in the name of the Son of God.' Believing in the name of the Son of God means passing from the ordinary, everyday name of this man, Jesus of Nazareth, to his eternal name, Christ, the name we all bear. It means knowing again and experiencing again that this life lived by a poor man, this life in struggle and suffering, is the truth for our life too. Nothing came to an end when he was tortured to death. Everything really only began, properly speaking. That is what we call resurrection.

A few years ago, at a conference in Italy, I got involved in a dispute with two other participants, both of them Catholic priests. I was irritated, because they said some things which seemed to me uncritical, anti-liberal and anti-Protestant. Finally I asked them: 'What have you really got against Protestantism?' They were silent for a moment, and then the elder of the two, who came from a little village in South Italy said: 'You feel just like us how difficult it is to be a Christian in the industrialized world. Christianity and the modern world are in a sense irreconcilable. We are completely agreed on this point. The only problem is the solution which you Protestants offer. You have changed religion in order to reconcile it with the modern world.' I have thought a great deal about that remark. Instead of changing religion until it fits the modern world, these priests wanted to change the modern world to make it fit the biblical view of life. Aren't they right?

I thought back to the years when I was studying theology in Göttingen, to my theological reading, to my work as a scripture teacher in schools, and as a writer on theology. What people did, essentially, in the Protestant faculties and churches was to adapt religion to the modern world. The modern world itself was thereby understood as being something fore-given; theology's task was to modernize the old religion and smooth down its rough edges. None of us theology students thought of trying to do things the other way round – of changing society until it was better adapted to the promise of the gospel and its vision of life. We never talked about the fact that the estrangement of men and women is a destructive social structure, and hence 'sin'. We only talked about the individual's rebellion against God. But this concept is extremely ill-adapted to describe sin in the real sense, the profound lack of faith of a young working woman, for example, who is not organized, whose hopes have been confined entirely to the private sphere. Where socio-economic questions were concerned, we abbreviated and diminished the concrete and precise things the Bible has to say. We didn't take biblical talk about the poor and the rich seriously. We spiritualized these concepts until they ceased to express anything concrete at all. It didn't occur to us that they had anything to do with finances, unpaid bills, arrears of rent, eviction orders and homelessness, with under-employment and unemployment, with lack of food or the wrong food, with hunger and sickness. We romanticized 'the poor'. We didn't describe them in bald words, like the country proletariat or war widows. We spiritualized the poor – and forgot them. Working people became invisible in theological circles. We knew nothing whatsoever about the conditions they lived in. We related sin to the rebellious personality, and no one taught us to think in collective categories. We cut off the idea of sin from our national history. All that had nothing to do with us as Germans in the twentieth century. We separated the guilt meticulously from our economy. We surmised what estrangement was, but we ontologized it into an eternal fate which was given with human existence. Thus we avoided calling the whole thing 'sin', and looking it in the face in the midst of our society.

We related the cross to the bearing of individual suffering. We cut it off from struggle. Indeed we didn't even see the crosses that stood round about us. And finally we thought about the resurrection only as we thought about a future life after death, in a different reality, instead of believing in it here and now as John did, when he talked in the present tense about our 'having life'.

This is perhaps somewhat of a caricature. But we have bourgeois theology in our bones, even if we think that rationally we have overcome some of its mythological concepts. What is left of the Christian tradition is colourless, and so are the images we have in our minds. They correspond to a dying civilization. Resurrection is associated with being reunited with one's loved ones, with coming home after a dangerous journey, with resting after a long day's work. The old biblical language talked about 'the city' of God, its golden gates, through which people could go in and out without hindrance, freely, a city in which people could talk openly about righteousness. But these pictures, which we find in the negro spirituals for example, have found no place in our civilization; and an 'enlightened' theology could do nothing to alter the fact. The change in the world of images tells us something about our diminished hope. What could once be talked about inclusively and as a whole had turned into an exhausted hope for an after-life. But it makes a difference whether we dream about peace and quiet or about happiness and truth. It makes a difference to the person who hopes whether he simply wants to be filled like an empty vessel, or whether he participates in the movement away from death. The middle-class culture changed religion instead of changing the world. We Protestants reduced our symbols and confined them to ourselves, to our personalities. We used religious concepts and images for one purpose only: they had to serve the supreme value of middle-class culture – individualism. When the beginning of all modern economic growth is the private initiative of the individual employer, and when collective forms of co-operation and shared property disappear through the economic process, then the prevailing religion is assigned the task of blessing this process. Religion becomes a tool of the ruling classes, and only continues to function in order to comfort the sad, enrich personal life, and give the individual the feeling of significance. Sin then becomes my personal transgressions, especially sexual ones. The cross then becomes my unique suffering, and the resurrection my individual immortality.

Even if I don't believe in life after death any more, the reduced religious question still remains fixed on a theme which is actually no longer ours at all. The real subject, the real discussion about the everyday and omnipresent death of the culture in which we live, continues to be avoided.

What does the forgotten resurrection mean? What statements can we make if we want to leave the prison of middle class theology? What language can we find to overcome middle-class theology at its heart, which is its individualism? There is a famous song belonging to the North American labour movement which deals with the workers' leader and song-writer Joe Hill. Joe Hill was arrested in January 1914 in Salt Lake City for alleged murder. In spite of world-wide protests and deep sympathy on the part of the public, he was executed in November 1919. The night before he was shot, a speaker at a meeting called out: 'Joe Hill will never die!' Twenty years later the following song was written about him:

> I dreamed I saw Joe Hill last night
> Alive as you and me.
> Says I, 'But Joe, you're ten years dead!'
> 'I never died,' says he.
> 'I never died,' says he.
>
> 'In Salt Lake, Joe, by God', says I,
> Him standing by my bed,
> 'They framed you on a murder charge.'
> Says Joe, 'But I ain't dead,'
> Says Joe, 'But I ain't dead.'
>
> 'The copper bosses killed you, Joe.
> They shot you, Joe,' says I
> 'Takes more than guns to kill a man,'

says Joe, 'I didn't die,'
says Joe, 'I didn't die.'

And standing there as big as life
and smiling with his eyes,
Joe says, 'What they forgot to kill
Went on to organize,
Went on to organize.'

'Joe Hill ain't dead,' he says to me,
'Joe Hill ain't never died.
Where working men are out on strike
Joe Hill is at their side,
Joe Hill is at their side.'

'From San Diego up to Maine
In every mine and mill,
Where workers strike and organize,'
Says he, 'You'll find Joe Hill.'
Says he, 'You'll find Joe Hill.'

I dreamed I saw Joe Hill last night
Alive as you and me.
Says I, 'But Joe, you're ten years dead.'
'I never died,' says he.
'I never died,' says he.

Let me try to present my theological interpretation of resurrection; it takes its origin from the biblical texts, but it is nourished and strengthened by other sources too. So I try to read the Bible in the light of Joe Hill who never died, and in the light of his brothers and sisters.

Nothing is so primal an expression of the Christian faith as the story of the resurrection. Christ has risen from the dead: that was and is a message of life-transforming power. It is the centre of the faith to which people have clung even under shattering conditions. There is such a thing as the reconciliation of estranged life; there is a victory over death and injustice. When in the Easter Eve liturgy we cry to each other 'Christ is risen! He is risen indeed!', then we are crying 'Liberation!' and we are one with tormented and shattered people, and one with the poor. 'He is risen', we say, and mean: we shall be filled, we love our mother the earth, we are building peace with the whole of our lives. We are beating swords into ploughshares. The power of what resurrection means must be felt in our own lives. We must again take possession of these words – resurrection, life from the dead, righteousness and justice – recognizing them as true on the basis of our own experience. Once we have given a name to our experience, we can describe our lives in the framework of the great symbols of our tradition: we too were in Egypt; we too know what Exodus means; we too know the jubilation of becoming free – of resurrection from the dead. Only the Christian experience we have made a part of our lives can be passed on, can be communicated to other people. But this power of the resurrection is veiled and remains unreal if we view Christ's resurrection in exclusive terms. If we make it an exclusive privilege of Christ's, then we miss its meaning, which is inclusive and means us all. To say that he is risen only has a point if we know that we too shall rise from the death in which we are now existing. He has left death behind him. But the decisive thing about this message is not an end in itself, not a complete, self-contained item of information.

There is a danger of falling victim to a theological heresy which the feminist theologian Mary Daly has aptly called 'Christolatry'. If we venerate Christ's resurrection without sharing in it, we are making an idol out of Christ, a fetish, which does not touch our own desolation. Sometimes I think that Christ is so homeless in the churches today because he finds worshippers there, but no friends. Too much adoration, too little fellowship. Because, admiring

Christ doesn't mean following him. Kierkegaard made that very clear to us. The worship of Christ without participation in his life, his sufferings and his death is the prevailing form of religion, at least in the First World. There are slogans – 'One way!', 'Jesus loves you!' 'Take Jesus!' – none of which offer anything with which to counter the prevailing individualism. These have a mass effect, but they are really harmless, a pattered formula, 'Lord, Lord', which does not express what that lordship means. Words like Jesus, obedience, love, faith, resurrection, remain completely untranslated in this religiosity, as if their meaning was above and apart from time, something once and for all; indeed it is not even felt necessary to say more precisely who Jesus is and why he is so important. Instead of being connected with experiences of liberation, steps towards righteousness and peace, he is set above reality as an authority. The authoritarian character of this piety justifies us in talking here about a kind of Christo-fascism.

It is the religion with which the usual kind of fascism can run its course, which unconsciously and helplessly works for fascism, by glorifying dependency; which believes itself to be non-political, but which really confirms forms of political power. The mania for adoring or worshipping power is not cured by writing 'Jesus' on one's banners instead of Hitler or Mussolini. The Christ of Christo-fascism doesn't suffer; he was never poor; or, if he was, that was unimportant – something purely external. He didn't perform his miracles in expectation of the kingdom of God, and organize people towards that goal; his actions were purely individual acts of help. This Jesus, in fact, loves you and you and you, but not us all. The Christ of the Christo-facists ended up on the cross, not for political reasons but for internal religious ones, because that was what his Father wanted. In this context the Bible isn't read as a materialistic book, which takes the human body seriously – its hunger, for example, and its society; instead it is idealistically spiritualized. The human-being-who-was-God acts in our stead. Worship, adoration, idolatry is the relationship to him which we can develop, not discipleship and participation.

But believing in Christ's resurrection doesn't mean heroic idolatry. It is precisely this which we can learn from the song about Joe Hill. I never died, said he. I am not dead. But these statements depend on his friends, on the people who carry on his cause. Resurrection as something purely objective, as a mere fact which would be true even without us, has no meaning. It would then only be a theological materialization under a positivist perspective of the world. The biblical witnesses are as far from this Christolatry and materialization as the people who sang about Joe Hill. Joe Hill, he in himself, he *a se*, to use a scholastic term, is dead. If individualism is our ultimate and most profound category for human beings, then we cannot understand what the resurrection is really about.

But anthropologically there is nothing which could be called Christ alone, he in himself. We are a part of Jesus Christ, and he belongs to our human existence, which cannot be defined by the limits of our body or in line with the uniqueness of our personalities, but through our social relationships. As people, we can be defined better through our relationships than through our substance. Our nature is a living relationship to others, a relationship resting on mutual help and sustained by an elemental need for communication. It is only in the capitalist concept of the person that we are reduced to monads whose relationship to the world is expressed in having, consuming and dominating.

We must free the idea of resurrection from the stranglehold of individualism. This also means that resurrection was not an event, an individual, isolated event which took place once, two thousand years ago. It must rather be understood as a process and it happens afresh, again and again, that people who were dead before rise again from the dead. Some people have already risen from the dead; if we remember them, we nourish our own hope of resurrection. This hope itself is unproven and unprovable. It is a genuine act of faith. The only possible proof of Christ's resurrection and our own would be a changed world, a world a little closer to the kingdom of God.

Resurrection gives us the beginning of the kingdom, not its completion. The pain of the unfulfilled promise is still with us. Christ bears the stigmata of his crucifixion on his body; in this sense the tradition itself witnesses to the difference between the resurrection and the kingdom of God, when the wounds are healed. So when we talk about liberation, we too mean an uncompleted process. By using this expression we are talking about the struggle for liberation which is itself liberating. We are not talking about freedom as a gift which we have received once and for all. In the concept of a permanent liberation, the cross and the resurrection are both present.

The resurrection is the symbol of faith. It is most profoundly encoded and it resists decipherment. Different periods have attempted different translations of this symbol. Whereas bourgeois theology stressed the individual dimension, the new theology which we are working on will stress the social dimension of the mystery. We link resurrection with liberation because our deepest need is not personal immortality but a life before death for everyone.

But is there a life before death of this kind? How could we describe it? Where does resurrection and liberation then take place? I believe that the strongest sign of the new life is solidarity. Where there is solidarity there is resurrection. When we break the neutrality of silence and abandon our complicity with injustice, the new life begins. People who earlier were invisible and forgotten become self-assured and find their own language. They stand up for their rights, and this revolt, this rebellion, is a sign of resurrection. I should like here to describe three elements of the new life: the new language, new forms of life-style, and new communities.

When zones of liberation emerge, people begin to talk a new language, in which the words 'mine' and 'yours' lose their meaning. One can make a whole list of words which belong to the language of the oppressor and are then replaced. In June 1976, school children in Soweto, South Africa, protested against the conditions in which they were living. The government had ordered that teaching in black schools should be given in Afrikaans. Mathematics, history and geography were to be taught in Afrikaans, a language which black teachers are as little proficient in as the black ghetto children. In those days, 15,000 school children marched through Soweto in protest. On their banners and placards was written: 'Do not force Afrikaans down our throats!', 'Our teachers can't teach in Afrikaans!', 'Afrikaans – the language of the oppressor!'

I believe we have all learnt the language of the oppressor. As a child I learnt Nazi German. Many of my North American friends were brought up with the cultural imperialism of Donald Duck. Our mass education takes place in the medium of advertising, which sullies every human emotion, because it presupposes that everything is for sale. Tenderness is something which the mild soap of a particular firm gives the skin. If anyone talks about the healthy, robust person, what he means is the person who is completely at the mercy of this power, who has surrendered his thinking and his feelings. We all grew up with the Afrikaans of the oppressor. We all have first to learn the language of liberation and, like every learning process, this one begins with a forgetting, a freeing from the mendacious language of children's television, the schools and the churches.

God is defined in the Christian tradition as love, as 'that very love with which we love one another', as St Augustine says. But in the language of the oppressor, in the Afrikaans of advertising which beats in on us, the word love is the definition of the relationship between a person and his car. And even if we use this word more seriously, it is reduced to the relationship between two people, cut off from the world and time. In our corrupted language, it often means no more than 'I'm OK, you're OK'; and this trivial middle-class game is increasingly passed off on us as 'God', even theologically. We are only capable of a disturbed, privatistic interpretation of love, and forget that God is the love which, as Juan Segundo says, forms 'human society in history'. The new language, which is a sign of resurrection, will teach us that God 'despite all our twisted and distorted images . . . is a God who is a *society*'.[1]

In this new language the existence of the individual will not have significance *in spite of* the senselessness of history and society, but *in accord with* history's meaning. The great educationalist Pestalozzi said at the beginning of the nineteenth century: 'There is no God and there is no belief in God as long as the suffering caused by injustice does not stop.' We cannot talk about God until we have become a part of the historical movement which ends suffering from injustice. We cannot talk about God until we have begun to be the agents, the subjects of this process of change called God.

The second thing I should like to mention is the new life-style which is lived in the islands of resurrection. A growing number of people are forming groups which are breaking with the old culture and rejecting its standards of education, career, income and way of living. The simplest form of solidarity with the poor is what the French worker priests in the 50s called 'presence': to be present, to share the life of the under-privileged, to be beside them in the struggle, to fight *with* them, not *for* them. The radical character of Jesus is a model for different life-styles like this. He ate and drank with whores; he gave up home and work; he developed a new language, which he and the poor found together and which was real for them, a very simple language of prayer and parable, which emerged from the context of their lives – the lives of the poor, the unemployed day-labourers, fishermen and housewives. The grass-roots congregations, which are growing up in Latin America and in some European countries too, are examples of the new life-style of the resurrection. The renunciation of middle-class privileges is part of this way of living. People work in co-operatives, that is to say without the specific forms of estranged labour. The groups read the gospels together and develop new forms of the spirituality of liberation, which rests on radical identification with the poor.

The new style of living, which we have first to search for, is connected with the new understanding of the surrender of our own lives. Surrender is both a spiritual and a political concept; the two experiences can no longer be separated from one another. To participate in the resurrection means that our lives don't lead towards what is dead, are not exposed to death's magnetic attraction. To be a Christian means that death is behind us. It no longer lies in wait for us. What awaits us is the love of which we are a part. As John says: 'We know that we have passed out of death into life, because we love the brethren' (I John 3.14). 'Out of death' is a description of normal, natural life. We must imagine the normal life of ordinary, middle-class people as being shot through with death. Its security is founded on dead capital; it acquires its mindless and inane joys from what is dead, from the possession and consumption of what is dead; its deepest anxieties are directed towards life's physical end. Possession, income, the kind of education that can be 'exploited', career and security are all supposed to cover up death; yet these things really only guarantee death's reality. By nature we live in death. It is only when we become capable of loving that we have 'passed out of death into life' and no longer need to fear, and no longer need to love, death's symbols – money, career, power. When death is behind us – which means the fear of death and the greed for what is dead – then the love into which we grow is ahead of us.

This brings me to the third sign of resurrection – the new forms of community. To build up community, to gain friends for the common cause, is not something which can be regulated by a division of labour, so that some Christians work as missionaries and others don't. The new life is lived only as a shared and extended life. The resurrection of Joe Hill is described in the simple words:

'What they forgot to kill
Went on to organize.'

Jesus sent out his friends to build the kingdom of God. He gave them exact information about the way they were to behave, such as having no shoes, having no second garment to change into, always going in twos. Where their organization was concerned, the most important instruction he gave them was the anti-hierarchical one:

You know that the rulers of the Gentiles lord it over them, and their great men exercise authority over them. It shall not be so among you; but whoever would be great among you must be your servant, and whoever would be first among you must be our slave; even as the Son of man came not to be served but to serve, and to give his life as a ransom for many (Matt. 20.25f.)

The reduction of privileges and domination is one criterion

for a liberated life. Jesus washed his disciples' feet – another sign of solidarity. The value of a member of the group is assessed, not according to his natural gifts or his social position in the group, but according to the question how this member meets people's needs.

What does resurrection mean for us? It means forgetting the language of the oppressor; it means a change in life-style; and it means new community. All these experiences which people have when they get involved with the cross are simultaneously political and theological changes. The radicalization is not divisible. To become more devout works out in practice in society as becoming more radical. Political radicalization also means new spirituality. I think it is a catastrophic mistake if in the Christian tradition we bring about a division of labour between those who fight and those who pray, those who risk action designed to change the world, and those who seek strength and renewal in prayer and reading the Bible. Struggle and contemplation belong together. A division of labour in this central self-expression of faith is deadly; it makes the people who fight blind and brutal, and the people who pray sentimental and deaf to the cries without.

In closing, let me try to say in how far the radicalization of faith has changed me and what has altered in my life through my growing into the movement of resistance and liberation.

First of all, my relationship to a whole series of people altered. Some old friendships broke up. Some neighbours stopped saying 'Good morning'. Some colleagues fell silent when I came into the room. On the one hand I grew lonelier. Jesus Christ doesn't merely free us and unite us, as the Nairobi slogan says;[2] he divides us too, and sometimes sends us out on paths which mean pain and isolation, conflict with our family, and estrangement from our social environment. On the other hand, my eyes were opened to many people whom I had never seen before. I came to know a new kind of community, one based not on aesthetics, personal preferences, or pleasure in what is beautiful, but on a common cause. In this sense the radicalization liberated me from old anxieties, because it created a new network of communications.

A second change for me was my understanding of history. Let me just link this with an everyday experience – opening the newspaper in the morning. It was something that always made me tired and sad. I felt that I didn't understand what was going on here or in other parts of the world. This helplessness is at the same time a kind of lack of conscience. But in the framework of the change I want to describe, this kind of helplessness and weakness is also a lack of faith. It is a capitulation before the objective cynicism of our situation. If we aren't capable of understanding our own history, then we can't see the significance of the struggle either. Our activities become a mere to-ing and fro-ing. We don't know why we visit this or that friend, why we watch this or that TV programme, why we do this or that with our time. Our work then becomes a senseless waste of time, only useful for making a living. But the more I understood my own share in the injustices of the social structure, the easier it became for me not to let myself be helplessly overwhelmed by the news in the papers, but to live more consciously and to choose between different activities. I have sometimes regretted losing some pleasure that has no special intention or purpose; because this belongs to the aesthetic existence of human beings. But in all seriousness, the beauty of Christ, if I may so express myself – that is to say, the beauty that doesn't exclude suffering and struggle – is preferable to the blind search for beauty which belongs to a middle-class aesthetic existence, Tradition, incidentally, expressed this fact by linking the love of beauty with the love of God, and rejecting, as incomplete and limited, unblemished beauty in which the struggles for righteousness have no share.

This change in my understanding of the historical situation also meant that my hope became stronger. It took on more flesh and blood. I was glad when a strike was won, or when a nation liberated itself. I learnt to read the newspaper in the interests of those without language and to listen at the very points where their voices were raised. In other words, God became more concrete for me. One of the theological questions which I had thought about for a long time was the relationship between power and love. As a woman, I quite naturally had difficulty with the idea of a mighty – indeed omnipotent supernatural lord, who was sometimes also called Father. I was not particularly interested in being ruled and protected by a heavenly sovereign of his kind. The idea of God which had been passed down to me by the fathers of the Christian tradition seemed essentially 'macho' – a man-God only for men. He was more interested in power than in anything else. Indeed he allegedly even wanted to be almighty. He was built up on the model of the free employer, who is independent of his workers. His titles – king, and so forth – insulted my democratic feelings, and the name 'Lord' was an affront to my solidarity with the people who always had to live under some master or other.

It was a long time before I was able to free myself from this God; and my path led me to a non-theistic theology, centred on the sufferings of the love of Christ. It was in this context that I wrote my first book, *Christ the Representative*.[3] The Son was closer to me than the Father, because he revealed what the Father was unable to communicate to me: love without privilege, love which empties itself and takes upon itself the form of a servant, of a member of the proletariat, love which prefers hell to heaven as long as other people are still condemned to be in hell.

I have tried to talk about God in a new way. The important thing for me is not merely to change the sexist language, by altering the pronouns we use for God. A world of female images and language can also be a world of domination and false protection. It is more important to overcome the inherited, substantial 'machismo' in talk about God, which means not making the bourgeois-male ideal our master. In my view, the adoration of power, the wish for absolute independence, is catastrophic, both theologically and politically. If today a central political goal for democrats is to achieve the co-determination of workers and their control over what they do, how can we endure talk about God which rests on the rejection of democratization and self-determination? If God cannot give up his power, we cannot trust him. If he doesn't want our liberation and our self-determination, then he is no better than, at most, a liberal capitalist. The God whom we need is not a private owner. There is only one legitimation of power, and that is to share it with others. Power which isn't shared – which, in other words, isn't transformed into love – is pure domination and oppression.

In the imprisonment of the old language, God is essentially separated from us, in the way that masters are separated from their servants, kings from their subjects, and independent employers from 'their' workers. Our present task is to express liberation in such a way that it doesn't take place from above downwards – that helpless objects are not just placed in some other situation by virtue of some heavenly intervention. No one can rise from the dead for anyone else; even Christ doesn't rise 'for us', but only as the first among many brothers and sisters.

There are times when we feel nothing of his resurrection – times of pain and torture, times of many crosses. In spite of that, let us not be among those who suppress the news of the resurrection or no longer believe in it ourselves. In times of many crosses we should go on telling what we have heard and understood. We should talk in such a way that Christ is missed, that he is even present as someone who is missing.[4] We should express the pain we feel when we don't perceive his victory; we should utter our longing. But to be missed is another way of being present. To have disappeared is a way of being there. Don't let us yield death an inch more than it already has. Let us talk about finding again what has disappeared, about the feeding of the hungry and about the resurrection of the dead.

In Auschwitz, from September 1943 to July 1944, there was a family concentration camp in which children lived who had been taken there from Theresienstadt and who – in order to mislead world opinion – wrote postcards. In this camp – and now comes a resurrection story – education in various forms was carried on. Children who were already destined for the gas chambers learnt French, mathematics and music. The teachers were completely clear about the hopelessness of the situation. Without a world themselves, they taught knowledge of the world. Exterminated themselves, they taught non-extermination and life. Humiliated themselves, they restored the dignity of human beings. Someone may say: 'But it didn't help them.' But so say the Gentiles. Let us rather say, 'It makes a difference.' Let us say, in terms solely of this world: 'God makes a difference.'

6 The Argentinian Context[1]

From 9 to 16 September 1979 I was in Buenos Aires, in order to deliver lectures in the Faculty of Protestant Theology there. For a whole week I lived and talked with the students and teaching staff of the Facultad de Teologia, which is supported by eight Protestant churches in Latin America. Just at this time the Inter-American Commission for Human Rights (CIDH) (which belongs to the Organization of American States) visited Argentine for the first time, in order to inform itself on the spot about people who had disappeared and been murdered, about prisons and concentration camps, torture centres and police terror. The fact that the commission came at all constituted a kind of resistance; for the first time the Argentinian press (and not only the English-language *Herald*) dealt daily in detail with the subject of human rights.

In Argentina there are three groups who are fighting for human rights. The oldest is the 'League for the Rights of Man', whose leadership is largely Communist. The 'Movimento Ecuménico' is a group supported by the churches, in which the former German La-Plata synod (EKaLP) also co-operated, The largest group is the 'Asamblea Permanente por los Derechos Humanos' (APDH), in which Jews, Catholics, Protestants and representatives of all political parties work together. Members of this group gathered together the material for the Inter-American Commission, collected statements of witnesses, lists and newspaper cuttings, with the help of which it can be proved that people who allegedly died in open clashes between the police and subversive groups were really in the hands of kidnappers months earlier. 'Talk about the double aspect of this', a representative of Asamblea Permanente urged me, 'Say what repression is doing to the Argentinian people, but say too what Argentinians are doing about it.' I will try to do both here. I myself listened to all the stories I am going to pass on to you. I heard them from the people involved, or from witnesses. Obviously I can't give the names of the people involved, or my authorities, or the places concerned.

Up to March 1977 the police still issued information about people who had been arrested. Since then this practice has ceased. A former student of mine introduced his sister to me. Her husband was interrogated by the police one Friday evening in his own home. On the Monday morning he wanted to go to work. She said, 'Stay at home – then we're together'. He thought that, since he had done nothing wrong or subversive, he ought to do his duty and go to work. 'He was a Peronist', Ernesto's sister added. So the daughter went to school, the son to work, the mother to her office, and the father left the house as well. That was two years ago. They never saw him again.

The woman who told me that was one of 5,580 people who have filed applications under the Habeas Corpus act. But it has to be assumed that the number of those who have disappeared is far larger, for all the people belonging to them are warned: 'If you want to see your husband again, don't take any action!' This silent terror is an important strategy on the part of the state terrorists. The people who have disappeared are exposed to it too. Some of them ring up their homes and say: 'Please don't make any enquiries about me. I'm as well as can be expected.

Don't talk to anyone!' Even of the few people who turn up again, not many are prepared to say what camps they were held in. They prefer to keep quiet about the torture they have undergone.

A Hungarian pastor knew a colonel in the police. When two of his friends disappeared, he asked this officer to find them. He was successful. The two men who had been imprisoned were told they had to leave the country. One of the two, a Jesuit, came to himself in a swamp near La Plata. He supposes that he had been given an injection, and then thrown out of a helicopter, unconscious. It was only after some hours that he was able to move again and to escape from the swamp. He rang up his Hungarian friend, was given a passport and left the country. He didn't want to talk about the torture that he had endured. 'If that happened among you', a representative of Asamblea said to us, 'you would use a computer to count the number and type of incidents.' In the middle of August 1979 the offices of the human rights groups were searched by the police. The judge who had ordered this investigation and the confiscation of the files gave as a pretext that contradictory evidence had arisen in Habeas Corpus proceedings. But after the investigation the judge did not return the files to their owners or to the police. He sent them to the army. The Asamblea is considering convening a jury to scrutinize this judge.

It is not by chance that these events took place just before the arrival of the Inter-American Commission. The intention was to make the work of the national groups for human rights more difficult. The families of the people who had disappeared were to be intimidated, and it was hoped that the delegates of the Organization of American States would be persuaded to cancel their visit. But the commission refused to be stopped. They talked to General Videla, visited various prisons and immediately made contact with the Asamblea Permanente, which at once felt itself appreciated and upheld.

The readiness of the regime to permit investigations of this kind is one of the contradictions of Argentinian reality. A member of the staff of the German embassy assured me that things were no longer so bad . . . Is Argentine on the way to a re-democratization? Some people think so. But the facts do not suggest it. Mr Cox of the *Buenos Aires Herald*, a paper which has for years reported infringements of human rights with courage and persevering fidelity, told me that again two people had disappeared. The relatives, however, had asked that their names should not be mentioned. Journalistically and legally, this is a report that cannot be utilized. It is of no value to any newspaper, or to the Commission for Human Rights, or even to the government. It is non-news about non-persons belonging to everyday Argentinian life. Two days later the front page of the *Herald* reported the disappearance of a whole family, including three little girls. This happened under the very nose of the International Commission, so to speak.

The government is trying to throw dust in the eyes of the public, both at home and abroad. At present it is doing so in three different ways, which at the beginning were not co-ordinated: with propaganda, with new laws, and with an increased silent terror. Well-meaning people really do believe that everything has improved. But in reality the oppression has only entered a different stage. It is now working with advertising experts, philosophers and lawyers, who are giving the cannibal face of state power a coat of powder and paint.

All the buses and many shop windows carry a cheerful blue and white sticker: '*Los Argentinos somos derechos y humanos*' – We Argentinians are upright and humane. This sticker first appeared when the Human Rights Commission came. It was a clever move. It conveys the impression that some foreigners or other are coming and maintaining that the Argentinians are inhuman and have no sense of justice. 'In reality', the slogan suggests, 'we simply love football and have at last brought order into our country.'

Another element in the propaganda has to do with geopolitics. The idea is to produce a sense of national territory. In the middle of the main street in Buenos Aires there are reproductions of boundary posts. 'Let's march to the frontiers!' is written on them. The border area, in which soldiers of course have to be stationed, is a favourite topic. School classes collect money for the poor people who live there. Plans for settling Argentinians in the border areas have been drawn up. The aim is to 'Argentinize' these sectors. Military and police (who are becoming increasingly indistinguishable from one another for ordinary people) are not only there for emergencies, not simply there in case of need. They exist to represent 'the common weal'. If enemies are not visibly present, they have to be invented. The Chileans are allegedly threatening the Argentinians. Geopolitics is a preparation for the ideology of national security, to which everything has to be subordinated. 'The state is the new religion we are living under', a theology student said to me.

All university professors and lecturers have to undergo two hours instruction in geopolitics from the military every week. In the schools any kind of critical thinking is unwelcome. Authors who could encourage it are replaced by others, from whom no such danger is to be feared. For the top classes in the secondary schools a new compulsory subject has been introduced under the title '*formación moral y cívica*', which is supposed to help the school children to conform to the prevailing doctrine of the state. The constitution is read word for word, though sometimes to the accompaniment of roars of laughter on the part of the school children. The state religion is intermixed with a

Thomist residue. Officially, the instruction has nothing to do with religion, but 'God' is viewed as a part of the national order. Anyone who doubts him is on the way to subversion.

During the Peronist era, there were books and other educational aids based on the methods of Paulo Freire. Children, and often grown-ups as well, learnt to spell and write the word 'milk', for example, by discussing the origin, nutritious value, distribution, price and scarcity of milk. A young teacher who had worked with this material earlier, took it to friends of mine a short time ago. She couldn't use it any longer, and it was too dangerous for her to have 'subversive material' in her own flat. All non-Catholic denominations had to register after the military *putsch* of 1976. One general put religion among subversive institutions, together with 'Marxism, Leninism and Judaism'. A fifteen-year-old Protestant girl refused to carry a picture of St Anne during a school fête. She was expelled from school and forbidden to attend any other school in the country. Later I learnt that this case had been reviewed and that she was now allowed to go to school again, in a place a long way away from the town where her parents lived.

Propaganda is at work too when the language has to be remodelled. Reflection is called subversion, helpfulness is sympathizing with subversion, peace is presented as war. 'We are in the middle of a dirty war', we are told in official government announcements. A priest who works in a slum, a *villa miserias*, said to me: 'What is going on here is officially called municipal reconstruction. We call it "eradicación". They carry it out by terror. They go through the area and tell the people living there: "You've got to get out." They cut off the electric light. They withdraw licences from the food shops. The shop-keepers are then the first to leave. Usually they have a piece of land somewhere else. The others follow – people who have saved up a bit and can buy a building site in another slum. Women living alone and children are the last to flee. Life is dying out here. There used to be football matches here on Sundays; we had youth clubs, and holidays and festivals used to be celebrated.' I asked what happened to the people who are the victims of this action. He shrugged his shoulders. There are tens of thousands of people whose few poor possessions diminish with every 'move'. At the same time Argentina generously takes in hundreds of Vietnamese refugees, while slum dwellers are often simply loaded into trucks and driven back over the border into Bolivia. These Bolivians, and others, will be back again a few months later, in another slum. They come simply because there is work there, even if the wages are well below the minimum necessary for existence.

In a bookshop I asked for poems by Juan Gelman known to me in translation (*So arbeitet die Hoffnung* – 'This is the Way Hope Works' – lyrics from the Argentinian resistance, edited and translated by Wolfgang Heuer). The young bookseller shook his head smilingly. I told him how much I liked Gelman's poetry. Then he went into a room behind the shop and came back with two books by Gelman, dating from the period before his exile. It really was a case of 'this is the way hope works', and nothing has ever reminded me so much of my childhood in Nazi Germany as this incident.

A further means of repression is provided by new laws. On 12 September 1979 a law came into force which permits a judge to declare a person dead after he had been missing for a year. The application can be made by relatives or by the state. This law has retroactive force to 1974. If no objection is made within 90 days, the missing person counts as dead. We discussed the advantages and disadvantages of the law with a journalist who was working for the *Herald*. He told us about a woman whose husband has been missing for three years. According to Argentinian law, children are not allowed to leave the country without the written consent of the father – not even permitted to cross the river into Uruguay, for a visit. The young woman said that she would go on looking for her husband, but the law allowed her and her children more freedom of movement.

The Junta has expressed highly contradictory views about the law. At one time it was said that the human rights groups had demanded a law of this kind. All three groups contradicted this vehemently. Only a few days before the law came into force, a government spokesman assured the Inter-American Commission that there was no intention of passing such a law. It is obvious that the disappearance of many thousands of people raises legal problems, and problems too of property and maintenance. In many cases the police have not merely looted houses, but have even made them over to other people. These encroachments on people's rights have also been reported to the government. But it is naive to assume that the law is intended to help men and women in their difficulties. The political interest of the Junta in this law is a quite different one. The people who have disappeared are to be forgotten once and for all. The past is to be buried – by law. The future is to be prepared for without the missing, after the long 'dirty war against subversion'. Legally speaking, the crux is the power of the judge; for it is not only the relatives who can apply to have a person declared dead – the state, in the form of the judge, can do so too. This is unique in the history of the administration of justice, and is in fact a new kind of 'final solution'. Cardinal Arns of São Paulo called the law one 'whereby the judges become the accomplices and agents of the murderers'.

Legal regulations do not always succeed in their purpose, thank God. The Argentinian trade unions were dissolved after the military *putsch* of 1976. At that time 80% of all industrial workers belonged to the unions. The idea was to intimidate them by demanding that they should register afresh with their respective factory managements. This attempt at intimidation was undermined: 85% of the workers registered. These are traces of resistance to terror, little signs and tokens directed against the superior force of the state.

'Have you joined the Communists?' a grocer asked the respectable middle-class couple who had been his customers for seventeen years. My friend answered: 'Jesus Christ was born in a little stable, not in a Sheraton Hotel. The woman who is staying with us with her baby has nowhere to live. We don't care what her views are. She needs help.' the shopkeeper listened attentively and nodded. He won't take any action against them.

It needs a great deal of courage not to be intimidated by the prevailing terror. The queue of people who wanted to hand in their petitions to the Human Rights Commission was a demonstration of this courage. For days the people stood five abreast; the queue of relatives was four blocks long; a moving demonstration on behalf of the lives of people who were to be declared dead. The secret police photographed the demonstrators. Passers-by abused them and secret agents made attempts at provocation. But there were also signs of sympathy and interest on the part of people who wanted to know what was going on.

The climate of terror is everywhere. The mother of a friend of mine told me that she had been asked by a North American group to visit prisoners in the notorious prison in Villa Devoto. She was prepared to do so, but her daughters urged her: 'You have seven grandchildren in the country!' 'I didn't do it,' she said, plagued by doubt, 'Was it wrong?'

There are stories of resistance, of neglected resistance, and of people who have broken under it. 'We had friends,' a lady told me, 'decent people, belonging to the Protestant church. They had three daughters. The two elder girls worked in a slum. They were full of idealism, you see – seventeen and eighteen years old. They joined one of those groups – you know what I mean. One night about three o'clock the secret police came to take them away. The older one screamed. She didn't want to be tortured. She took a pill and committed suicide. The younger girl was taken away. She has been missing ever since. Think of the parents! One daughter dead, another disappeared. The third girl is still alive.'

Torture during interrogation is the rule, not the exception. Methods are used which leave no trace. Don Jaime Smirgelt of the Asamblea Permanente says that there hasn't been a single person who has escaped this torture. The army, the navy, the air force and the police have refined their methods. As a NATO general remarked, these methods are a combination of what the OAS did in Algeria and what the CIA did in Vietnam. Prisoner's clothes are taken away from them and they are put under a cold shower for 15 minutes in winter. Afterwards they have to lie down on the floor of their cell and are beaten. This method leaves no bruises – which means that it leaves no evidence. The prisoners are given 20 to 100 strokes on their heels. Many people have died under these tortures.

The government tries to legitimate the terror on the grounds that this is 'the dirty war against subversion', against the extreme left, against the Monteneros, against the terrorists. I read in the newspaper a pro-government denunciation of left-wing terror which was signed by 300 relatives of victims. The statement stressed that, before the military dictatorship, no one could feel safe from bombs and explosions on the streets. According to the highest estimates, the terror of these groups cost the lives of about a thousand people. Prominent people were especially endangered – industrial leaders, the heads of the police and the army, and politicians. The present government declares regretfully that this subversive terror has forced them to use dirty methods too. But now, this newspaper statement stresses, Argentina has peace and order at last.

But this explanation of the situation is inadequate. It is contradictory, because according to this retaliatory logic, state terror should long since have come to an end. Propaganda and laws alone evidently do not constitute sufficient repression. Other explanations have to be found for the terror exerted by the state and the continued systematic torture. For it is not merely a matter of the excesses of a few crazed sadists. Economic necessity comes into it too. What are the economic foundations of the repression? Ever since the military takeover, wages have sunk, practically speaking, by at least half. Both the trade unions and the national association of industrial owners were dissolved. As isolated, localized groups, the unions have practically lost all their power. In the opinion of the minister for economic affairs, Martin de Hoz, national industry is not efficient enough. The people, he maintains, simply don't work hard enough and must consequently be exposed to international competition, so that they can adjust to it.

This economic policy can be seen in concrete terms in everyday life. Everywhere one sees advertisements in the shops citing the sole remaining definition of quality: import. All restrictions on imports have been lifted in order to make national industry competitive. According to the opinion of the economic leaders (who appeal to Milton Friedman of Chicago), the home market is inadequate. The liberalization of imports leads practically to the shattering of industry. A trade union leader said that the work of four generations of middle-class people was being destroyed here. When the smaller firms go bankrupt, the multinational concerns buy them up.

The destruction of organized labour is a prerequisite for

all these manoeuvres. Terror was already needed when the wages of the workers, who had been organized for generations, were cut by half. In recent years there have been continual unofficial strikes, go-slows and walk-outs in Argentina. At the beginning of June 1979 a railway strike paralysed the whole transport system round Buenos Aires. There was resistance, so there had to be terror. According to the plans of the minister for economic affairs, Argentina was supposed to play the role envisaged for it in the international division of labour worked out by the trilateral commission. It was to develop an agricultural production progressive enough to tie up with the international agribusiness. The economics minister plans an increased economic concentration and monopolization of industry. The multinationals are to be given preference when credits are granted and in investment policy. Financial dependency on the World Bank and the International Monetary Fund (whose executive bodies are dominated by the United States) is to increase. It is against the background of these economic plans, which wipe local industry off the map and throw back the history of the country by fifty years, that the present repression has to be seen. The ban on thinking and the persecution of psychiatrists and lawyers who resist are not the only expressions of this mockery of human rights. An organized working class cannot be tolerated. The middle level of management in the working-class movement has been liquidated. It is true that in Argentina – unlike Chile – a few trade union and left-wing party bosses have been spared, but only so that the attack on the level below them could be all the more deadly. The Soviet Union is a powerful trade partner of Argentina's. It doesn't lift a finger for the men and women who work there.

A young teacher was working in a *villa miserias*, a slum, and was given a present of school material: exercise books, pencils, books. Sometimes she found a bank note slipped into an exercise book, and she used this to buy other material for the children. She was taken away and condemned to eight years imprisonment, on the grounds that the school had been supported by the Monteneros.

In the days when the overtired members of the Commission on Human Rights were receiving the relatives of people who had disappeared, when other people were disappearing and being tortured, we discussed in the Faculty of Theology the question of faith as the struggle against objective cynicism. Under this heading, I tried to describe the situation in the industrial West. What I said was accepted and given a new stress. 'Objective cynicism is organized here', one student said. 'They have a very clear and effective strategy. The question is: what have we? What is the cost of discipleship, the cost of following Jesus?' 'For me, terror', said another. 'This is the fear that paralyses me. The very moment we ask: "What did the missing person do?" we are already beginning to justify the terror.' Another student said, 'We are dominated by a vast schizophrenia. We don't practise what we preach. You need a lot of faith to believe that the 100,000 who have disappeared are right.' Still another added: 'We are living under the cross. We are going to be crucified, and we are covering ourselves up with the pleasures of football.' 'It is a time of repentance, not resistance,' said a pastor. 'We have collaborated. We weren't motivated by Christ. It is time that the church became the church, that it uttered a prophetic word against lies and violence.' A professor said: 'Resistance is the ethos of European theology, but that is bound up with a particular historical situation, at the end of a long historical project which is out of date. The New Testament doesn't only talk about the cross. Out of its certainty of overcoming (*trionfo*) it also talks about what Christ did and lived. The essential thing is to create a new situation in the church; the theology of liberation has been converted into pastoral theology.'

I have tried to sum up the main headings of these theological discussions in Argentina. Two main trends emerge from them. Some people say: 'Our analysis was inadequate. In 1966 the theology of liberation was still the theme of the moment. But when I heard about the young people who were tortured and then thrown into the sea, I asked myself: What has happened? Was our theory wrong? We haven't grasped the reality. The instruments used for the analysis were insufficient. We didn't reach the whole, the total Christ. The analysis remained too general and too uninterested in the individual.' The others, generally older students, said: 'The instruments of the analysis must be in conformity with Christ's. Attempts to start from the total and integral Christ are mistaken. The historical subject of our churches is the middle class and it is as middle-class people that we are pursuing theology. But the question is, for whom we are pursuing it, and whether we are with the poor and start from them.' Here I was reminded of the conversation with the priest in the slum, who himself only told me of one disappearance. But hardly any of the people who worked with him – social workers, teachers, priests, doctors, lawyers, young people – are still there. They have disappeared, been tortured, sentenced to imprisonment, or have emigrated. This observation tallies with those made in trade union circles. Cautiously formulated, and with reservation, it may be said that it is the articulate section of the lower middle classes who have been liquidated by the repression, as helpers of the helpers. But what does this tell us about the majority of the Protestant churches – the German-speaking congregations, for instance, about whom a student cried despairingly: 'They don't want to change. A grass-roots community is one based on resistance against an estranged, de-personalized world. It isn't our analysis that is at fault, but our practice, which is bound up with particular congregational structures.'

So we were on the search once more for a new church, for its historical subject, even if we thought we were now able to perceive its historical project somewhat more clearly. Another part of the discussion was headed 'our Father and Mother in heaven'. In a culture where *machismo* is a matter of course and is deeply rooted in the subconscious – a culture of the masculine man, whose relations to women are built up on feelings of superiority, rule and subjection – this discussion of a feminist theology, made by women for women, of course evoked perplexity and embarrassment.

'God doesn't need theology', said a student, 'But we need the reflection which helps us to live our faith.' Can this reflection exist without the experience of resistance? 'Conflict is the great teacher', said Che Guevara, who according to some theologians is an Old Testament figure. If this is true, then many Christians are living in the Old Testament today, in resistance, in suffering and in hope.

Here is a story from Chile. A Presbyterian minister from South Chile distributed food which he had been given by friends in North America. He was arrested and taken to Los Alamas prison in Santiago. A hundred and fifty men were living there in a room the size of an institute library. He took over the role of chaplain and held daily devotions and Bible study for his fellow-prisoners, most of them socialists. He had never had a congregation like that, he said. When he was released the other prisoners wrote their names on his back with burnt matches. It was November and warm. He got out without being stripped and searched, and went to the Peace Committee. Most of the names – names of people who were listed as having disappeared – were still legible.

The names turn up, written with burnt matches on a

prisoner's back. The hour of silence is at an end, Don Jaime Smirgelt told us. For the first time, political parties in Argentina – the Peronists and the radicals – have identified themselves with the cause of human rights. These are signs of hope, which cannot be blotted out by the threat of torture, the terror of silence or even by the softer terror of oblivion.

NOTES

1 Faith as a Struggle against Objective Cynicism

1. M. Buber, *Tales of the Hasidim: The Later Masters*, Eng. trs., Schocken Books 1948, p. 315.

2. Cf. P. P. Pasolini, *Freibeuterschriften. Die Zerstörung der Kultur des einzelnen durch die Konsumgesellschaft*, Berlin 1978 (a translation of 1978 selections from *Scritti corsari*, Milan 1975).

3. Here and for ch. 4 of the present book cf. also my contribution in H. Habermas (ed.), *Stichworte zur 'Geistigen Situation der Zeit'*, Frankfurt 1979.

4. Cf. the weekly newspaper *Die Zeit*, No. 30, 21 July 1979.

5. P. P. Pasolini, op. cit., p. 89.

2 Sin and Estrangement

1. R. D. Laing, *Do You Love Me? An Entertainment in Conversation and Prose*, Pantheon Books 1976.

2. The following pages, down to p. 29, form the final section (pp. 31–36) of my essay 'Der Mensch zwischen Geist und Materie. Warum und in welchem Sinne muss die Theologie materialistisch sein?' in *Der Gott der kleinen Leute. Sozialgeschichtliche Bibelauslegungen, Band 2 Neues Testament*, ed. W. Schottroff and W. Stegemann, Chr. Kaiser Verlag, Munich, Burckhardthaus-Laetare Verlag, Gelnhausen Berlin Stein, 1979.

3. E. Käsemann, *An die Römer*, Tübingen, 1973, p. 168; Eng. trs., *Epistle to the Romans*, Eerdmans and SCM Press, 1980, p. 176 (altered).

4. E. Käsemann, *Perspectives on Paul*, Eng. trs. SCM Press and Fortress Press 1971, p. 21.

5. Ibid.

Notes

6. J. Harder (ed.), *Christoph Blumhardt–Worte*, Wuppertal 1972, p. 111.

7. Cf. Günter Altner, *Leidenschaft für das Ganze, Zwischen Weltflucht und Machbarkeitswahn*, Stuttgart 1980, pp. 18f.

8. The story is the last but one in *Dreams by a French Fireside*, Eng. trs., Chapman and Hall 1886.

3 Cross and Liberation

1. This lecture was first delivered on 7 October 1977, in Paris, on the occasion of the conferring of an honorary doctorate by the Free Faculty of Protestant Theology. The text appeared in *Junge Kirche. Eine Zeitschrift europäischer Christen*, February 1978.

2. Walter Jens, *Am Anfang der Stall – am Ende der Galgen: Jesus von Nazareth*, Stuttgart 1972. The German text is as follows:

> Wer mir folgen will,
> nehmen den Balken auf sich,
> an dem man ihn kreuzigen wird,
> Denn wer sein Leben behalten will,
> wird es verlieren,
> doch wer es um meinetwillen verliert,
> der wird es behalten.

3. *Das Neue Testament* translated by Jörg Zink, 8th ed., Stuttgart 1975. The German text is as follows:

Wenn jemand meinen Weg gehen will, denke er nicht an sich selbst und sehe von seinem eigenen Leben ab. Er nehme den Kreuzbalken, an den sie ihn hängen werden, auf seine Schulter und gehe hinter mir her. Wer nämlich sein Leben retten will, wird es dabei verlieren, wer aber sein Leben verliert, weil er zu mir gehört und weil er meiner Botschaft glaubt, wird das wahre Leben finden.

4. These lines appear in Ira D. Sankey's *Sacred Songs and Solos, with Standard Hymns, combined,* and other late nineteenth-century hymnbooks, attached as a refrain to Isaac Watts' hymn, 'I'm not ashamed to own my Lord'.

4 Christ – the Dignity of Men and Women

1. P. P. Pasolini, *Freibeuterschriften*, p. 31.
2. Ibid., p. 46.
3. From here the text of this chapter, apart from a few additions, follows the text of my essay 'Christ bin ich wegen Christus' in the collection *Warum ich Christ bin*, ed. Walter Jens, Kindler Verlag, Munich 1979.
4. J. D. Salinger, *Franny and Zooey*, Little, Brown and Co. 1955, Heinemann 1962, pp. 198ff.

5 Resurrection and Liberation

1. Juan Luis Segundo, SJ, *Our Idea of God* (A Theology for Artisans of a New Humanity 3), Orbis Books 1974, Gill and Macmillan 1980, p. 66.
2. The slogan of the Fifth Assembly of the World Council of Churches which met at Nairobi, Kenya, in November 1975.
3. Dorothy Soelle, *Christ the Representative: An Essay in Theology after the 'Death of God'*, Eng. trs., SCM Press and Fortress Press 1967.
4. According to conservative estimates, 15,000 people have disappeared in Argentina since the military take-over on 24 March 1976.

6 The Argentinian Context

1. This report appeared under the title 'Fussball und Folter wie gehabt', in *Junge Kirche, Eine Zeitschrift europäischer Christen*, December 1979.